W9-BWA-292

# Home Office, Work, and Utility Spaces
## Remodeling Projects

David H. Jacobs, Jr.

## TAB Books
### Division of McGraw-Hill, Inc.
New York  San Francisco  Washington, D.C.  Auckland  Bogotá
Caracas  Lisbon  London  Madrid  Mexico City  Milan
Montreal  New Delhi  San Juan  Singapore
Sydney  Tokyo  Toronto

643.7
Jac
c1

**Disclaimer**
The home improvement designs and views expressed by the author are not necessarily approved by Makita USA, Inc. Makita USA, Inc., shall not be held liable in any way for any action arising from the contents of this book, including, but not limited to, damage or bodily injury caused, in whole or in part, by the recommendations or advice contained herein.

©1995 by **McGraw-Hill, Inc.**
Published by TAB Books, a division of McGraw-Hill, Inc.

Printed in the United States of America. All rights reserved . The publisher takes no responsibility for the use of any of the materials or methods described in this book, nor for the products thereof.

pbk   1 2 3 4 5 6 7 8 9 0 DOH/DOH 9 9 8 7 6 5 4

Product or brand names used in this book may be trade names or trademarks. Where we believe that there may be proprietary claims to such trade names or trademarks, the name has been used with an initial capital or it has been capitalized in the style used by the name claimant. Regardless of the capitalization used, all such names have been used in an editorial manner without any intent to convey endorsement of or other affiliation with the name claimant. Neither the author nor the publisher intends to express any judgment as to the validity or legal status of any such proprietary claims.

**Library of Congress Cataloging-in-Publication Data**
Jacobs, David H.
    Home office, work, and utility spaces : remodeling projects  / by
  David H. Jacobs, Jr.
      p.    cm.
    Includes bibliographical references and index.
    ISBN 0-07-032406-9 (pbk.)
    1. Dwellings—Remodeling—Amateurs' manuals.  2. Offices—Design
and construction—Amateurs' manuals.  3. Utility rooms—Design and
construction—Amateurs' manuals.  I. Title.
TH4816.J36  1994
643'.7—dc20                                                   94-40463
                                                                  CIP

Acquisitions editor: April Nolan
Editorial team: Yvonne Yoder, Book Editor
                David M. McCandless, Managing Editor
                Joanne Slike, Executive Editor
Production team: Katherine G. Brown, Director
                Ollie Harmon, Coding
                Jan Fisher, Desktop Operator
                Nancy K. Mickley, Proofreading
                Joann Woy, Indexer                          0324069
Designer: Jaclyn J. Boone                                    HT1

3/95

CONTENTS

## Acknowledgments

Throughout the course of this book endeavor, I have been most fortunate to receive an overwhelming amount of support from many special people, companies, and organizations. I very much want to thank them and acknowledge their participation.

Jack Hori, senior vice president, and Roy Thompson, product marketing manager, for Makita USA, Inc., have provided outstanding assistance. Their avid interest and genuine encouragement is most appreciated and elevated even higher by the superior service I continue to receive from their tools.

I want to thank Francis Hummel, director of marketing for The Stanley Works, for his contributions to this project. Working with Stanley hand tools and other products is a pleasure, as they always come through with excellent performance and efficiency.

David Martel is the marketing manager for Central Purchasing, Inc. (Harbor Freight Tools). He has been instrumental in a number of different ways and I thank him for his interest and support. Harbor Freight Tools catalogs are chocked full of goodies and I recommend you request one.

Eagle Windows and Doors manufactures products that are easy to install, hold up under the most adverse conditions, look great, and offer a great deal of energy efficiency. I want to thank Tom Tracy, advertising manager, and John Stearns, manager of the showroom in Bellevue, Washington, for their support.

I am grateful for the support provided by Thomas Marsh, vice president of marketing, and Daryl Hower, business manager, for Leslie-Locke. Their roof windows, skylights, heat ducting materials, and other products are easy to install and always perform as expected.

Hilarie Meyer, associate merchandising manager for Campbell Hausfeld, has been most helpful. I appreciate her support and the amount of work that was saved by the performance of Campbell Hausfeld's pneumatic nailers and other quality tools.

I would also like to extend my most heartfelt appreciation to the following people and the companies or organizations they represent: Maryann Olson, project coordinator/public relations for the American Plywood Association; Betty Talley, manager of marketing services, and Jeff Barnes for American Tool Companies, Inc.; Tina Alexiess, product manager for Autodesk Retail Products; Patricia McGirr, marketing manager for Alta Industries; Victor Lopez, technical service manager for Behr Process Corporation; Don Meucci, marketing director for the Cedar Shake and Shingle Bureau; Kim Garretson and Rich Sharp for DAP, Inc.; Jim Roadcap for The Eastwood Company; Matt Ragland, marketing manager for Empire Brush, Inc.; Jim Brewer, marketing manager for Freud; Mike Cunningham, director of corporate communications for General Cable Company (Romex ®);

Peter Fetterer, director of public affairs for Kohler Company; Dave Shanahan, director of marketing for Keller Industries, Inc.; Mario Mattich, director of public relations for Leviton Manufacturing Company, Inc.; Peter Wallace, senior vice president for McGuire-Nicholas Company, Inc.; Ruth Tudor, product publicity manager for NuTone; Jim Schmiedeskamp and Phyllis Camesano for Owens-Corning Fiberglas Insulation; Mr. Dana Young, vice president of marketing for PanelLift Telpro, Inc.; Greg Hook, communications manager for PlumbShop; Bill Cork, public relations manager for Plano Molding Company; Bob McCully, vice president of sales and marketing for Power Products Company (SIMKAR); Rob Guzikowski, marketing manager for Simpson Strong-Tie Connector Company, Inc.; Jim Richeson, President of Sta-Put Color Pegs; Dick Warden, general manager for Structron Corporation; Marty Sennett for DuPont Tyvek;

Beth Wintermantel, marketing communications manager for Weiser Lock; Timm Locke, product and publicity manager for the Western Wood Products Association; Philip Martin, product marketing manager for Häfele America Company; Karin

Martin, marketing services supervisor, and Jeff Bucar, marketing manager for Halo Lighting; Robert Suarez, sales manager for Quality Doors; Matthew Smith, marketing manager for U.S. Ceramic Tile Company; Sue Gomez, marketing customer service manager for Zircon Corporation; Elvi Tarien, assistant to the president for PFAFF American Sales Corporation; and Dan Murphy, director of marketing for Dritz Corporation.

I must also thank Brian Lord, Bob Greer, Jim Yocum, John Gittings, Steve Hayes, Josh Pearson, and Ken Whitehair for their hands-on help and ever entertaining words of wisdom and encouragement. Van and Kim Nordquist came through with another excellent job of developing hundreds of photographic prints, and I thank Scott Wakeford and Al Davis from the Mercer Island, Washington, Building Department for their patience and advice.

As always, my family deserves recognition in many ways. So, I thank my wife, Janna, for her expertise at the computer and for running so many errands, and our children and growing family of sons-in-law, grandchildren, and close friends; Nicholas, Luke, Bethany, Ashleigh, Matthew, Adam, Brittany, Courtney, Kirsten, Shannon, Joey, Terri, Steve, Whitney, Tyler, Daniel Dodson, Ryan Stearns, and Steve Emanuels.

Finally, I must thank Kim Tabor, editor-in chief, April Nolan, acquisitions editor, Sally Straight, acquisitions assistant, and the entire editorial staff of TAB/McGraw-Hill for all of their encouragement and support.

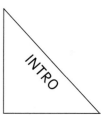

Two SCHOOLS OF THOUGHT are generally contemplated with regard to workspaces that always seem to be clean and tidy; either the person who is supposed to use that space doesn't do much work or there just isn't enough work to keep that worker busy. Think about it. How many times has your office, work, or utility space looked like a tornado has hit it once you have completed a major project?

Now, I am not advocating that we hard workers with plenty to do celebrate the fact that our work areas might look like the pits, but simply want to acknowledge that it is almost impossible to keep offices, work, and utility spaces in pristine condition all of the time. However, lots can be done to our home work areas to make them more convenient, efficient, and organized, and make them much more visually attractive.

The primary purpose of any home office, work, or utility space, is to provide its homeowner with an area where specific tasks may be accomplished safely and effectively. Therefore, first considerations should revolve around the types of work that are expected to be undertaken in your work areas and then design functional accessories that will assist those activities.

For example, a beautifully built wide counter unit mounted about 36 to 40 inches off of the floor might well serve a 6-foot person as an excellent drafting table, but would be totally impractical for a seamstress who wants to sit down and must be able to reach a sewing machine pedal with her foot. Likewise, while bright lighting in active crafts spaces might be most appreciated, the ability to slightly dim lights in office settings might help make it easier to see data printed on computer screens and also reduce eye strain for computer operators.

Once you have decided to refurbish a basement into a viable work or craft center, remodel an existing laundry or utility room, or turn a vacated bedroom into a home office, take plenty of time to consider just exactly what kinds of options are available. When rooms are empty, walls opened up, and floors bare, the time is perfect for installing pipes for a central vacuum system, recessed ceiling lights, intercom or sound system speakers, television cables, and so on. Once you have completed your home improvement project, it is doubtful that you will look kindly upon poking holes in new walls and ceilings for the installation of those things you overlooked.

Deciding upon which kinds of accessories you want to install in a home office, work, or utility space might be confusing; as a huge variety of fixtures, appliances, and amenities are widely available. Allow yourself plenty of time to shop around and browse through home improvement centers, office supply outlets, and appliance showrooms, to become familiar with the various work center arrangements that are on display. Bring paper and a pencil along to jot down notes and outlines of those set-ups you find most appealing.

*Home Office, Work, & Utility Spaces* is designed to show you how to build and install a variety of different accessories that will enhance your activities in those home spaces. In lieu of pages simply filled with photos of finished rooms, this book describes and demonstrates how various things are built from the ground up, and then installed and finished. You are encouraged to safely use the methods and techniques illustrated on the following pages to build and install those accessories that will suit the needs of you and your family and help to organize all of your home work centers.

This book is certainly not intended to be the last word on home offices, work, and utility spaces. Rather, it offers basic information on how home work center accessories are assembled. Once you have a solid grasp of the basics, use your imagination to build custom amenities utilizing different types of wood, trim, molding, and other materials that will make your home office, work, or utility space look great and help you keep those spaces organized, safe, and efficient.

# Designs & ideas

## CHAPTER 1

JUST ABOUT EVERYONE has dreams of converting some nook in their home to an office, workspace, or utility area. Do-it-yourself buffs create plenty of designs in their heads that they consider to be ideal. But just how detailed are those dream designs? Are they simply images of tidy, attractive, or elaborate areas in their homes? Or are they thorough plans that include work centers, accessories, and storage units? Do the fixtures take full advantage of all available space, and are they built to dimensions that most ideally fit the physical sizes of the persons who plan to use them?

Don't lose sight of the details you want to incorporate in your dream workspace, but hold them at bay while you create your primary workspace design. The major differences between plain and gorgeous work areas rest in the types of material employed, the amount and style of trim and molding installed, the color of paint or stain applied, and the decor options (such as curtains, blinds, floor and wall coverings) that surround the room.

Basic workspace assemblies, like counters, shelves, and bookcases, are also easily embellished. You can give simple plywood storage units real eye appeal by using oak plywood and adorning them with oak trim and molding. Apply a quality sealer and stain; install attractive handles, pulls, or knobs. The result is a classy shelving unit or bookcase that might have cost hundreds of dollars at a fine furniture store.

At first glance, the bookshelf on the next page looks totally disorganized, untidy, and just plain ugly. Although it is messy and unsightly, this home office is functional. It has served as a viable workspace where volumes of work have been successfully completed. Home office, work, and utility spaces must first be designed to accommodate and enhance labor efforts.

After basic floor plans and essential accessory items have been figured into the design, homeowners can begin considering options for making shelves, bookcases, counters, and other units visually attractive and suited to the home's decor.

## Primary workspace considerations

The bookshelf in the illustration, made from rough CDX plywood, could be replaced with an attractive, sturdy unit built out of A-grade hardwood plywood, like birch or oak. Then it could be trimmed with comparable molding. An additional unit to the left could help reduce the amount of clutter scattered about the desk area. Another filing tray would be useful.

Shelves, bookcases, cupboards, counters, drawers, and cabinets all serve as storage facilities. Open shelves should be saved for items you want to display. Cupboards (shelves with doors, normally located on upper wall areas) are ideal for keeping things out of sight. Drawers are great for small items. Cabinets and work counters generally provide ample space for storing large items.

Use paper and pencil to draw out different floor plans for your workspace. What do you need the most, storage or counter space? What counter height is best for you? Desk tops ordinarily rest about 30 inches above the floor, counters around 36 inches. Kitchen cupboards are usually 16 to 18 inches above countertops. Would that space leave you enough room for the activities you have planned for that area? Cupboards are

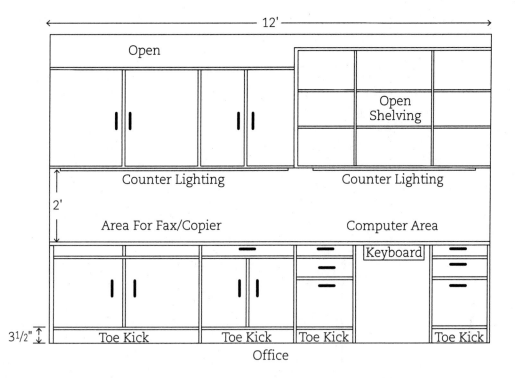

Office

generally 1 foot or so deep, while countertops extend out from walls 24 to 30 inches.

Measure different areas around your home to get an idea of which dimensions are most comfortable for you. Are your kitchen counters set at a height that would also be perfect for a workbench? Does the height of your dining table make it a comfortable work area for writing or sewing? Take your tape measure to an office supply outlet and measure different desks on display. Make note of the dimensions you find most comfortable. For laundry rooms, measure the washer and dryer to see if counters installed next to them would be functional for you if they were built at the same height.

The utility room serves as a center of operations for many household tasks. Laundry duties, sewing ventures, and craft projects fill the room with an abundance of supplies and material. Storage is a primary consideration. Perhaps your

## Workspace & storage ideas

utility room offers enough wall space for the installation of a 24-inch-deep, floor-to-ceiling storage unit—about the size of most clothes closets. Shelves could be complemented by an adjacent open area for hanging clothes in need of mending.

A few ¾-inch dowels slipped horizontally into U-shaped brackets are perfect for storing rolls of ribbon. Insert dowels into wooden bases for vertical storage. Measure the items you expect to place in storage areas. Build the shelves to accommodate those items, with an inch or so extra to facilitate maneuvering. Better yet, design storage units that allow shelves to be adjusted at different heights.

Work Study/Sewing
Arrangement for
a 6-Foot
Closet Conversion

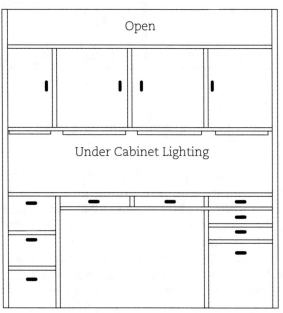

Modified clothes closets make ideal work centers. Outfit one with shelves and a counter to create a handy sewing center or office space. Under-cabinet lighting will do an excellent job of illuminating the countertop. An electrical outlet is easy to install if you can tap into an existing receptacle on the other side of the wall.

4    *Home office, work, and utility spaces*

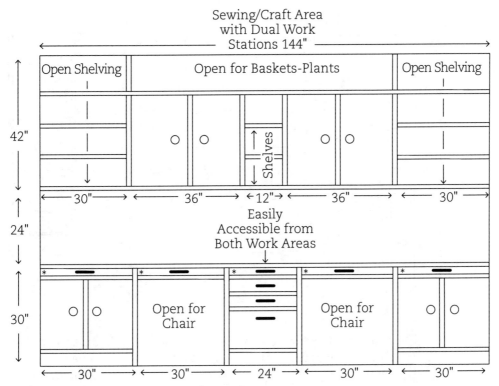

Sewing/Craft Area
with Dual Work
Stations 144"

Open Shelving

Open for Baskets-Plants

Open Shelving

42"

Shelves

30"    36"    12"    36"    30"

24"

Easily
Accessible from
Both Work Areas

30"

Open for
Chair

Open for
Chair

30"    30"    24"    30"    30"

* Note Narrow Top Drawers for Notions

An organized system of cupboards, shelves, cabinets, and counters will provide a wealth of storage and workspace. Many bedrooms have at least one solid wall that measures 10 to 12 feet in length. A vacated bedroom, therefore, could easily support a full-wall work area that is 24 to 30 inches deep, and still have plenty of room for a guest bed and dresser. Design open areas for chairs around existing electrical outlets to avoid the extra work required to relocate them.

Corner workspaces serve multiple functions when they are designed to allow two or three people to work on separate projects at the same time and in the same space. For example, set up a computer center on the left and a sewing area toward the right. For crafts and hobbies, outfit one side with tools and supplies needed for general crafts and the other with specific implements used for special hobbies.

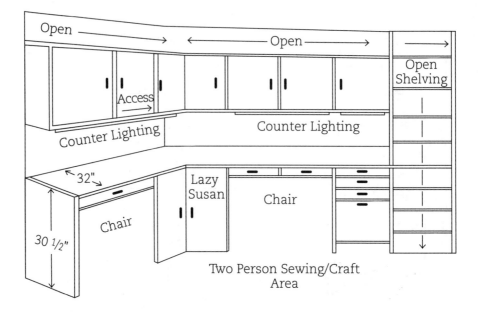

Open ⟶ ⟵ Open ⟶ ⟶

Access ⟶

Open Shelving

Counter Lighting          Counter Lighting

32"

30 1/2"          Chair          Lazy Susan          Chair

Two Person Sewing/Craft Area

Again, build your work center and storage cupboards to heights that are most comfortable for the person who will be using them. It might be impossible for shorter family members to reach shelves close to the ceiling. Unless you have items for storage that will be used infrequently, consider leaving a foot or so open for displaying baskets and other colorful objects.

6   *Home office, work, and utility spaces*

The homeowner who created the arrangement on page 6 receives lots of compliments for his efforts. He built and designed this home workspace in his 34-x-26-foot garage. Cabinet and cupboard floors, tops, and side panels were made with ACX plywood. He made the doors from AB birch hardwood plywood, and fixed the counters at 36 inches above the floor and covered them with laminate. The mobile work center rests on locking wheels and is topped with 2-x-2-inch Douglas fir boards laminated together. The mobile unit features a wide lip that extends out far enough to comfortably accommodate him as he works while sitting on a stool. The workspace is used for crafts, home repair projects, general storage, and even some office work.

Storage continues toward the right with four more cupboards and a 4-foot-wide closet that stretches from floor to ceiling. To the left is a small counter/sink unit. This entire project covers about 60 linear feet. Including the sink and faucet, the builder figures he spent about $1,200 for materials. A similar grouping purchased through a retail outlet and then installed by a professional contractor could cost as much as $10,000 or more.

Plans for a variety of handy, mobile work stations are available through the American Plywood Association. Cost is minimal, so you should request a catalog that lists all of them. Plans are also available through the Western Wood Products Association. Addresses and telephone numbers for both of these associations are listed at the end of this book, in the sources section.

## Locating building plans

Most home improvement and do-it-yourself magazines frequently feature articles about building home work centers, and many of these articles include plans. Lots of companies also advertise plans for a wide variety of home improvement projects, including desks, counters, cupboards, and cabinets. Most magazines are available through libraries, where articles are cataloged on microfiche for easy retrieval.

Active do-it-yourselfers commonly discover new designs for home office and workspace accessories by browsing through home improvement centers, office supply outlets, and furniture stores. They carry a small 10- or 12-foot tape measure, a piece of paper, and a pencil. When they find an interesting item, they

# Home Shop

A. Multipurpose Worktable

B. Multipurpose Workbench

C. Workbench Storage Cabinet

D. Foldaway Vise Table and Sawhorse

inspect it closely, noting specific length, width, and height dimensions. They also look at different joints to see how boards are fitted and secured.

Children need tables, counters, and workbenches built to accommodate their small stature for working on hobby, craft, or school projects. A work center built just for kids in a basement or utility room, outfitted with tools and supplies commensurate with their abilities and maturity, will help them derive more enjoyment from their creative endeavors. Likewise, a desk area and chair that has been built for their comfort will go a long way toward helping them stay focused on homework and other school studies.

Most furniture outlets include showroom areas that feature items designed for children. In fact, some companies even specialize in children's furniture. Stores like these are ideal for learning about modern designs of workspaces and desk areas just for kids.

## Workspace amenity ideas

Heavy-duty drawer guides on the kitchen pantry unit on page 10 provide plenty of support for storing small kitchen appliances: blenders, slow cookers, toasters, pressure cookers, and so on. This design is also perfect for hobby and craft areas where portable tools require rugged support. Sliding shelf/drawers like these can hold scroll saws, jig saws, belt/disc sanders, and lots of other tools. Items placed on such shelves are easier to find and replace, since they do not need to be pulled from deep, lower base cabinets with fixed shelves.

Pegboard has been around for many years. For a while, folks seemed to frown on it as a way to store tools. One reason was that the metal hooks were notorious for falling out of the holes every time a tool was picked up. That problem was solved with the invention of pegs that stay in place. These plastic hooks feature a protrusion on the shaft that snaps into the pegboard directly beneath the hole that houses the top of the hook. As shown on page 11, they are available in different colors and shapes, are very strong, and can be pulled out and moved with ease.

Nothing brightens up a workspace better than rich sunlight and fresh air. If your office, work, or utility space is located on the top floor, or your home is on a single level, seriously consider ventilating with a roof window. The model on page 11

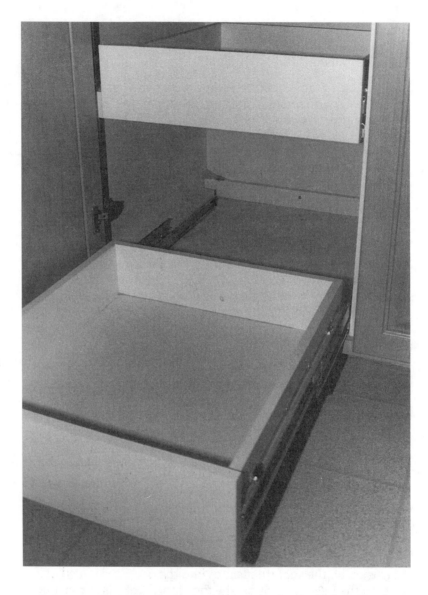

was very easy to install. Optional accessories include a shade that can be pulled over the glass to block direct sunlight and a long pole for operating the windowlatch from below.

Smoke detectors save lives. Plan to install one in your new workspace. If your workspace will be frequently filled with sanding dust and other airborne debris from hobby activities,

opt for a heat detector instead of a smoke detector. Smoke detectors are very sensitive to airborne particles; they will activate if dust reaches the sensors. Heat detectors, on the other hand, are designed to sense (and then activate) when the room temperature increases sufficiently. They will not generally react to dust or other particles in the air.

## Summary

Workspace designs must originate with your personal preferences, your needs, and your home's available space. A simple way to start planning your new work area is to sit in a corner of the project room with a pad of graph paper, a pencil, and a tape measure. Draw the floor plan of the room to scale on the graph paper, with each square representing 6 inches, (two squares to each foot). For laundry rooms, measure the amount of space your washer and dryer require and pencil those dimensions into the area where you want them. Then, draw in counters, mobile work or storage spaces, and anything else that will require floor space. Allow for 3-foot aisles and at least 4 feet behind chairs.

With a floor plan completed, work on walls. How many open shelves, bookcases, or cupboards do you want or need? Will a section of countertop need open space above it for access to a photo enlarger in your new darkroom? Will your hobby activities involve tall items that require plenty of maneuvering space? Draw in all of the tools and other objects you expect to use on your new workspace counter and be sure their measurements are accurate. You don't have to be an artist and actually draw different things, but at least pencil in rectangles that represent the amount of space those items will occupy.

Once you have formulated a complete set of plans for outfitting your new office, work, or utility space, take a trip to your local home improvement center, office supply outlet, or furniture store and look at the many different styles of accessories that are available. From inspecting them, you should be able to decide on a definite style and learn what types of materials to employ in your accessories.

By putting together a viable workspace plan that accommodates your needs, and then building it with carefully selected materials and options, you can make your home office, work, or utility space dream a reality.

# Tools & materials

## CHAPTER 2

PROJECTS PROGRESS SMOOTHLY and efficiently when quality tools are operated safely, in accordance with manufacturers' instructions. Power tools always pose serious threats of injury, and must be used with caution. Be certain work pieces are securely clamped in place. Always wear safety goggles, and roll up sleeves. Do not allow other clothing items to hang freely, especially near power tools.

Cheap tools from bargain stores cannot provide the same level of service as the more expensive, precision-made models. Inexpensive, lightweight screwdrivers will not withstand continuous use and will wear out quickly when used to twist screws into hardwood boards. Other mediocre tools respond similarly to tough jobs.

The tools and equipment featured in this book were selected because of their high quality and rugged durability: they performed as expected, job after job.

Home improvement centers are full of all sorts of materials and supplies. Although most of these outlets carry large inventories of dimensional and other wood products, you might have to shop at a specialty lumberyard for the best selections of hardwoods and other wood species. Most telephone directories list various suppliers of hardwoods, tile, floor coverings, and other materials in the yellow pages.

Dimensional lumber, like 2 × 4s, 2 × 6s, and so on, actually measure differently than their listed size. The 2 × 4s really measure 1½ × 3½ inches; 2 × 6s are 1½ × 5½ inches. Be sure to measure the length of each board before using it, too. An 8-foot board might actually be 8 feet and ¾ inch long or more.

Smaller boards, like 1 × 4s, really measure ¾ × 3½ inches wide. Remember these figures while you design different workspace accessories to keep mistakes at an absolute minimum.

**Tools**  Keeping saw blades sharp and clean is almost as important as following strict safety guidelines and operating instructions. Dull blades will cut unevenly. Sharp blades, however, leave cut edges smooth and square; then, when you mate one piece of wood to another, the joints are nearly invisible.

A variety of different saw blades are designed for specific types of wood cutting. Blades with the most teeth generally cut the smoothest and are preferred for cabinetmaking and other finishing jobs, while blades with fewer teeth are designed for jobs requiring lots of repeated cuts in dimensional lumber. They are used when precision is not nearly as crucial—such as when cutting studs for wood-framed structures.

This Makita 10-inch Slide Compound Saw is a handy tool. It can cut boards up to 12 inches wide. The power head can be rotated in two different directions to effect compound cuts—board ends that are cut at angles both vertically and horizontally. Equipped with a sharp clean blade, this saw also does an excellent job cutting rails and stiles (face trim pieces) for cabinets, cupboards, and similar units.

You will need a circular saw and guide to cut panels out of plywood. A table saw could be used, but you should employ roller stands and a helper to assist you in handling full sheets. The best tool for cutting plywood is a panel saw. You can also have plywood cut to your specifications at your local home improvement center.

All wooden objects must be sanded before applying sealer, paint, or stain. An assortment of sanders is available. Use a heavy-duty belt sander for quickly knocking down highly uneven surfaces or smoothing wide panels.

Orbital and finish sanders are employed for lighter jobs to get surfaces perfectly smooth. A small belt sander can be used in tight quarters.

Sandpaper is available in sheets of different grades. Sheets are labeled by numbers, with the lowest numbers representing the coarsest grits. A #60 will be very coarse and is used for heavy sanding jobs, while the #100 and #240 are much finer and are used for finish work.

Along with sandpaper sheets, discs and small rectangular pieces are available for power sanders. Some sanders hold the paper in place by way of clips. Others, like the orbital model, incorporate a hook-and-loop system. The sander base is covered with a hooking material. The backs of the sandpaper discs are coated with a looping material. The system works very much like a common hook-and-loop clothing or shoe fastener.

Serious woodworkers rely on planers and jointers to make rough wood smooth and slightly bowed wood perfectly square. This combination planer/jointer was used to turn a rough chunk of oak dunnage into a beautiful piece of wood that was then routed, sanded, and stained. It will be used as a backsplash for a counter/sink unit.

## Fasteners

Building and installing cabinets, cupboards, and counters requires the use of fasteners. All-purpose screws, commonly referred to and used as drywall screws, are very versatile. Use them to secure panels together where screw heads will not be seen, like behind or under cabinet units.

Finishing nails feature very small heads. They are used to secure rails, stiles, and trim pieces. Their small heads are then punched below wood surfaces to create a small hole, to be filled with putty and sanded so that it appears that nails were never used.

Totally different fasteners are employed to secure shelves or cabinets to walls in the absence of studs. The fastener at the top of the illustration has a plastic body and is simply screwed into drywall with a Phillips-head screwdriver. It creates its own hole with a sharp tip and then holds tight with wide threads that spiral around the shaft. A separate metal screw is then inserted through a workpiece and into the plastic fastener.

Second in line is a toggle bolt. A hole of specified size is drilled into drywall and the bolt inserted into it. Tightening the featured screw causes ribs on the fastener body to expand out, eventually clamping itself to the wall. Similar toggle bolts are available that do not require drilled holes; they are designed to be forced through walls with a hammer.

The last fastener is a plastic anchor. After a hole is drilled in a wall, the anchor is pushed into position. Once a screw is inserted and torqued down, the anchor body splits in half to wedge itself inside the hole.

The Häfele America Company's catalog is large enough to be bound as a hardback book. Along with drawer trays, storage baskets, computer convenience products, and a host of other items, Häfele America offers an amazing array of furniture hardware products.

Fasteners used for furniture are completely different than those used to secure things to walls. Look at a prefabricated particleboard desk or work center; you will notice that special fasteners hold panels securely together. Some are simple brackets. Others involve pin and cam mechanisms. Häfele displays at home improvement centers include drawer guides, furniture fasteners, and lots of other useful products.

## Materials

Plywood is strong, versatile, and readily available. It is rated according to surface finish and smoothness. Letters designate plywood grades. The letter A denotes the smoothest, while the B grade is usually featured on the opposite side of A for high-quality grades of hardwood plywood. The C grade is rougher and might include a few knot holes, and D is the roughest, with probably lots of knot holes in the top plies. If the letter X follows grading letters on a piece of plywood, an exterior glue was used to manufacture the sheet.

Regular plywood is made from soft woods, like Douglas fir, hemlock, pine, etc. A number of thin plies glued together form sheets from ⅛ to 1¼ inch thick. The most commonly stocked plywood is ACX and CDX grades in varying thicknesses. Plan to use ¾-inch ACX for interior cupboard panels, shelves, and floors.

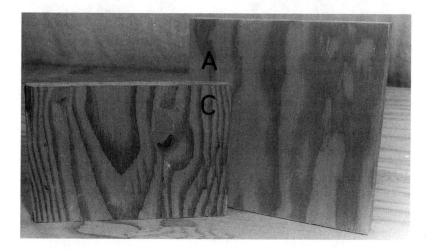

For applications where appearance is of utmost concern, use hardwood plywood. Birch plywood takes paint and stain very well, while oak plywood is very attractive. Hardwood plywood will cost nearly twice as much as softwood plywood, but the results will be more than twice as appealing.

If you decide to make your own cupboard and cabinet doors out of plywood, use hardwood plywood. It will accept paint and stain much better, and its edges will not be filled with voids where knotholes were located near inner plies.

Although plywood doors might look fine for some garage and basement work centers, home office and workspace fixtures need solid-wood panel doors.

Making panel doors requires lots of time, patience, and experience. Some cabinetry companies, however, provide a very easy and quite economical alternative: solid wood custom cabinet and cupboard doors designed to fit your specific installation. All you have to do is supply the companies with the desired dimensions, and they will build your doors in the style you select. Some companies also manufacture custom drawer fronts to match doors.

Quality Doors specializes in supplying cabinet refacing materials. Along with doors and drawers fronts, it offers real wood veneers with adhesive backs that simply adhere to cabinets and cupboards. Thin hardwood plywood panels are also available in custom sizes, and are used to cover exposed cabinet end panels. Quality Doors offers a video tape that fully explains how to reface cabinets, hang doors, and order materials.

All paints, stains, and sealers are not equal in quality. Some brands do not cover nearly as smoothly and effectively as others. Follow application instructions to the letter while painting or staining to achieve the high-quality finish you expect. Most products include labels with definitive application instructions. Paint is available in quart, gallon, and 5-gallon containers; it can be mixed to create any color you desire.

Drywall primer sealer is specifically designed to seal new drywall material in preparation for coats of latex paint. An undercoat or primer must be used on bare walls before the application of enamel paint. Primers seal bare surfaces and allow paint to adhere and cover much better. Save yourself a lot of extra work by applying primers before painting. If you don't, your paint job will neither look as good nor last as long.

The variety of interior and exterior housepaint colors available is astounding. Get paint chip cards where paint is sold. Bring some home to see which colors will blend best with your furnishings and decor.

Condition bare wood before painting or staining. Conditioners seal wood and cause it to swell a bit. Use a fine grit sandpaper to smooth any irregularities, carefully remove all sanding dust, and then apply the stain according to label instructions. Finish the stain by applying a finish sealer, like polyurethane. This will protect wood and its color finish for a very long time.

The HousePainter from Campbell Hausfeld is an airless machine designed to spray paint through a nozzle. It is usually used outdoors, but you can still paint interior walls quickly and easily without ever having to stoop over to dip a roller into a pan of paint by using their PaintPro Roller. The roller attachment screws onto the HousePainter handle in place of the spray nozzle. This unit is equipped to draw paint from both 1- and 5-gallon paint containers.

In lieu of paint over interior drywall, you might prefer wood applications. Wood paneling is available in 4-x-8-foot sheets, small 4- to 6-inch cedar strips about 2 feet long, and in tongue-and-groove boards at random lengths in cedar, pine, and other species.

Tile companies offer a wide range of tiles in different sizes and shapes. Some designs are installed in a specific manner to create a three-dimensional effect. Consider tile for countertops around utility sinks and on adjacent walls.

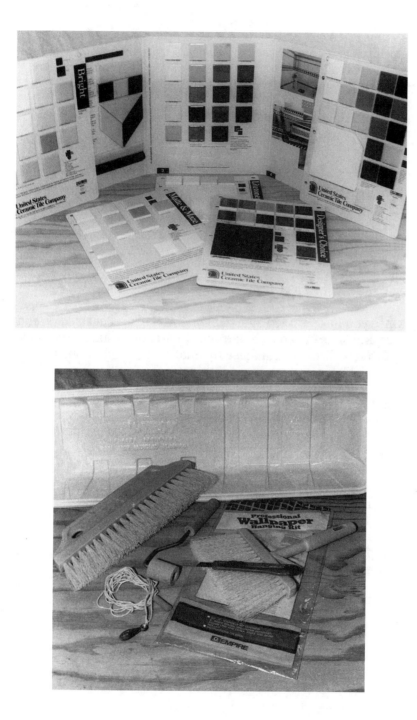

Wallpaper is available in non-pasted and pre-pasted rolls. Each has pros and cons. Representatives at wallpaper stores will be able to explain which type of material is best suited for the application you have in mind. All of the tools you'll need to hang wallpaper are included in the handy kit from Empire Brush Company shown on the previous page. The kit includes brushes, a seam roller, a razor knife, and a chalk line used to make perfectly vertical lines on walls for reference points.

## Summary

If you are planning a full-scale remodeling project to turn an old utility room into a modern work center, a vacated bedroom into a bona fide home office, or an unfinished basement into a multi-purpose craft/sewing center, establish a budget before jumping in with both feet. Construction and finishing materials have gone up in price over the last couple of years. You might hiccup when you see that oak plywood costs well over $50 a sheet.

Once you have arrived at a viable floor plan and decided on the size and style of cabinets and counters, shop around to see how much it will cost to purchase the materials. In addition, if you prefer to have professional contractors tackle plumbing and electrical work, ask three or four to give you cost estimates. If you find that your plans have gone way over budget, don't feel too bad. It happens to just about everybody.

Scale plans down to fit your budget as necessary. Consider alternative materials, or divide the overall project into sections that can be completed over an extended time frame. For example, complete the framing, electrical, plumbing, wall and floor finish work; then outfit one entire wall with its accessories during the first phase. Each following phase should completely outfit one wall, until all phases are finished and the entire job is done to your satisfaction.

# Demolition &
# new construction

ANY TIME YOU START tearing out parts of your house, expect messes. Airborne dust will filter through openings around doors and travel inside heat ducts to eventually settle in other rooms on furniture, shelves, and so on. Attempt to minimize dust problems by sealing off interior doorways with plastic sheets and masking tape.

The construction of a home addition is considered a major improvement endeavor. Whole books have been written about building foundations, floors, walls, roofs, etc. This section will lightly touch on a few tasks involved with those processes.

An entire house wing does not have to be torn down to make way for remodeling a room. However, you will have to remove baseboard molding, floor coverings, and portions of drywall.

## Demolition for room remodeling

The basement on previous page in this 1940s vintage house had not been updated for decades. Water problems, a lack of electrical outlets, and other factors made it easy for the homeowner to decide to gut the basement and start remodeling from bare studs.

He sealed off the upper floors by securing a sheet of plastic over the doorway with masking tape. He made arrangements to dispose of all the debris before demolition began. Disposal was a major concern. Not all refuse areas or transfer stations are equipped to handle construction materials.

A new exterior door now stands in place of the old one. It is surrounded by freshly painted drywall and handsome recessed ceiling lights. What a difference!

Once you have elected to gut a room down to bare studs, take time to contemplate all of the amenities you would like to eventually have in that space. Even though you might not be able to afford an intercom system now, for example, you should run the wires for it in your gutted room so that they will be in place when you are finally able to install one. The same goes for television cables and sound system speaker wiring.

Heavy, textured popcorn ceilings were the rage a couple of decades ago. They are not considered fashionable today. Fortunately, they are quite easy to remove, although very messy. In rooms with carpet, roll a sheet of heavy 4- or 6-mil plastic over the entire floor and tape it in place along all edges. Then use a squirt bottle to drench the ceiling; gently scrape away the textured material with a wide putty knife.

In rooms with bare concrete floors, you might even consider spraying the ceiling with a mist from a garden hose. Be sure you have a wet/dry vacuum on hand to pick up excess water. Apply the putty knife with a gentle touch. Wet texture comes off like warm butter. If you have to scrape harder, and the texture is dry and powdery, stop and soak the material again with water. Texture that falls to the floor will be the consistency of mud.

Some contractors apply a thin bead of white caulking along the top edges of white baseboards next to white walls. This helps to hide gaps between walls and baseboard materials. Use a sharp

razor knife to cut caulking before pulling baseboards away from walls. If you don't, the caulking will cause drywall paper to peel off the wall.

As shown on the next page, use a wide-bladed bar to pull baseboards away from walls. Start them with a little persuasion from a hammer. Then, operate the bar in a horizontal direction so that any impressions it makes in the drywall will be covered later with new baseboard material. Never pull up on the bar. This causes dents in drywall above the baseboards that will have to be filled with drywall compound and sanded smooth.

Carpet is held in place with strips of wood bearing lots of tacks. The pointed ends of these tacks face upward to catch carpeting and hold it in place. Tack strips are secured to wooden floors with regular nails and to concrete with concrete nails. These nails are partially driven into the tack strips. Use a pry bar to break strips free. Be very careful while handling them; the points on the tacks are extremely sharp.

Carpet seams are held together with heat-activated glue strips. Note that a heat gun is carefully used to loosen glue so one section of carpet can be removed. *Caution:* heat guns are capable of developing extremely high temperatures—hot enough to ignite normal combustible materials. For this task, the gun control was turned down to about half capacity. Tension was maintained on the carpet so that it would release from the strip the moment the glue softened. Note that the operator is wearing a heavy leather glove to protect her hand from burns.

Once secured, drywall is a very sturdy material. While it is being handled, however, it is quite fragile, and will crack if carelessly maneuvered. Drywall consists of a solidly packed gypsum material sandwiched between layers of heavy-duty paper on each side. Only one side is to be exposed. You can recognize that side by sighting down the long edges to notice how they taper and become thinner. These tapers are designed to hold drywall compound, allowing finishing efforts to produce smooth, relatively flat surfaces.

Use a hammer to poke a hole in drywall for removing material. Be sure to wear safety goggles. Wear a dust mask, too.

Make the hole big enough for your hand to fit through. Then, probe the open area with your hand to locate electrical wires, plumbing pipe, and any other obstructions as on next page. Once you are certain that the area is clear, use a drywall saw to cut along ceiling joists or wall studs.

If you come across a section of wire, pipe, or other object, break off the section of drywall already cut and then carefully maneuver around the obstruction, taking pains not to cut into it. Drywall removal creates a great deal of gypsum dust. Wear a dust mask, and keep exterior windows and doors open for ventilation. Seal off all interior openings with plastic and tape.

## Cutting out drywall

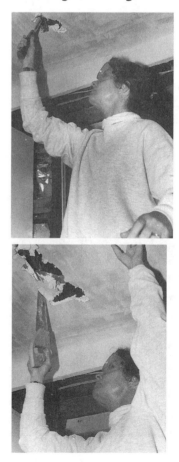

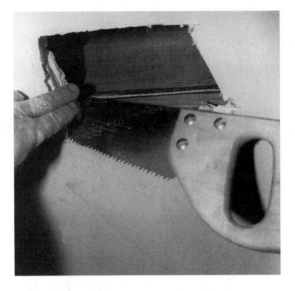

## New construction

New interior house walls are built with 2 × 4s. If the area where you want to build is in a room complete with a ceiling, you will only have to erect walls. Install and secure horizontal top and bottom plates first, and then toe-nail studs one at a time. In some circumstances, you can build the wall frameworks on the floor and then tip them up into place as entire units. A few careful taps with a sledge hammer forces them into place.

Bottom plates secure easily to concrete floors with anchors. This rotary hammer makes quick work of drilling a hole through the plate and into the concrete. A threaded anchor will be tapped into place and then a nut torqued down to wedge the fastener solidly into position.

Concrete foundations that protrude into living spaces pose special problems. One of the best ways to cover such foundation sections is with furring strips. On page 29, 2 × 4s are used to essentially erect a miniature wood-framed wall on the inside face of the foundation. Drywall is then nailed or screwed to it. Concrete anchors also work quite well for these strips, although countersink holes must be drilled in the wood strips. The anchors must sink below the wood surface so they do not obstruct the drywall.

Once the new addition to your home has been framed and roofed, seal exterior walls. For years, contractors used 15-pound building paper for this purpose. Today, homeowners are much better off using Tyvek Housewrap. This material is very sturdy and comes in 9-foot-wide rolls. It seals walls to prevent air from leaking through any openings between wall sheathing. Installation requires the cooperation of two people. The material is secured to wall studs with special nails that feature extra large washer-like heads.

## New home addition considerations

## Windows

Tyvek is rolled out to completely cover the walls. After it has been secured, it is cut and wrapped around window and door openings. In lieu of Tyvek, 15-pound building paper must be wrapped around window and door openings before those units are installed. This illustration depicts a young builder nailing down a small shim to prepare for an Eagle window installation. Every window company has specific guidelines installers must follow with regard to the rough opening dimensions required. Shims are used to keep windows off the sills and to help builders get them perfectly level.

Window installations typically require two people; one on the outside to hold the window in place and one on the inside to set shims and ensure level positioning. Windows scheduled for installation in a second-story addition require at least three workers. Two carry the unit up sturdy ladders and one completes interior tasks.

Windows are equipped with nailing flanges. Nails are inserted through bottom and side flanges, then driven into sills and studs. Nails at the top are started above flanges, driven into studs part way, and then bent over the flanges. This way, if headers above windows bow down over time, they cannot cause windows to bow or buckle. In this illustration, two nails at the top flange were used to keep the window in place while its position was checked with a level on the inside; they were removed and correctly positioned once the bottom and side flanges were secured.

This window is equipped with its own trim, the boards that surround the inner window space. Other windows do not have trim. You must finish off that area with wood or drywall. The gap that exists between the trim and rough window opening should be filled with expanding foam. This material will seal off the gap to prevent the loss of heated interior air during cold winter months.

## Doors

All kinds of doors are available at home improvement centers, some lumberyards, and door manufacturers' showrooms. Doors can be purchased separately or complete with jambs. Inexpensive models feature door knob holes located in the middle so that doors can be installed for right- or left-hand opening. Higher quality doors are designed specifically for right- or left-hand opening. Your preference must be conveyed to door dealers so they can supply appropriate units.

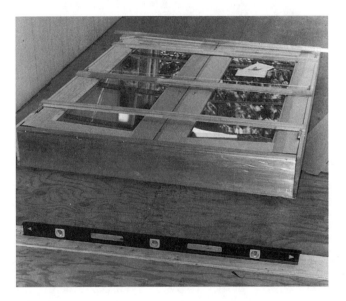

This door, positioned flat on its exterior side and complete with jamb and threshold, is securely packaged. A worker will screw a metal nailing flange into place while the door remains in this position to prepare it for installation. A 4-foot level is used to verify that the rough opening threshold is perfectly level. If not, shims will be employed to make this piece of ½-inch plywood level so that the door threshold will rest on it correctly.

Use pieces of tapered cedar shakes as shims to fill gaps between the door edge and rough framing studs. Place them at the spots where door hinges are located. Once the door has been set to perfection vertically and horizontally, drive large screws through the hinge and door jamb and into the stud for a secure application.

Eagle doors are equipped with special hinges that allow installers to make fine-tuning adjustments after the doors have been hung. A hex-head wrench turns the adjusting hinge screws, making the door move slightly to attain a perfect fit between jambs and alignment with its mate.

Insulation is rated by R-values. Simply stated, the higher the R-value, the thicker the material. Different regions of the country require specific R-values in exterior home walls and ceiling spaces. The requirements for desert areas in Arizona are much less than they are for North Dakota. Check with your local building department to learn what the requirements are in your area.

## Insulation

Do yourself a favor when you run electrical wire for your new addition. Position it low to the bottom plate; remember that 16d nails that are 3⅓ inches long have been driven through plates and into the stud ends. By running wire about 4 to 5 inches above the bottom plate, you can easily separate layers of insulation and fit them around the wire.

When insulation is cut and installed, fine fibers separate from the batts and become airborne. For that reason, you must follow recommended procedures. Wear long sleeves, gloves, safety goggles, and a dust mask. A cap or hat is a good idea, too. Cut insulation with a sharp razor knife. First cut the paper moisture barrier, then make second and third passes to cut the fiberglass material.

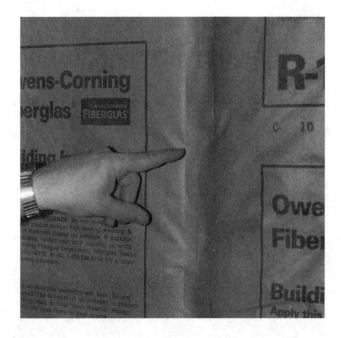

Paper moisture-barrier material is placed on the interior side of walls. Flaps on both sides fold out to make it easy to staple them to wall studs. Owens-Corning Fiberglass Insulation is available in widths to accommodate standard wall studs placed 16 inches on center, and ceiling joists placed 24 inches on center. Purchase batts in widths that will accommodate your project.

Cover floor joists with ¾-inch plywood tongue-and-groove subfloor sheets. Place them ⅛ inch apart to allow for expansion and contraction. To maintain that ⅛-inch gap, simply tap 8d nails along installed sheet edges; these nails have a diameter of about ⅛ inch. Place a bead of subfloor adhesive along joist tops before installing plywood. Attach the plywood to the joists with deck screws.

Older homes might feature 1-inch-wide boards placed at an angle across floor joists in lieu of plywood material. If your remodeling job consists of renovating an old room with such subflooring material, take time to securely screw the subfloor to the joists with deck screws. This helps a great deal to eliminate potential floor squeaks. Once the subfloor has been secured, cover it with 15-pound building paper in preparation for the underlayment installation.

Underlayment material is positioned on top of subfloors for rooms that will eventually be covered with floor vinyl or carpeting. Tile floors require ½-inch ACX plywood underlayment. Hardwood floors are placed on top of subfloor materials.

Typically, subfloors are constructed with ¾-inch material. Underlayment usually measures ½ inch, for a total floor thickness of 1¼ inch. However, some applications have been made with ¾-inch subfloor and ¾-inch-thick hardwood materials. To match this height in an adjoining laundry or utility room scheduled for floor vinyl, you might have to use ¾-inch underlayment.

## Summary

Thinking through your remodeling efforts before starting them will help you prepare for the jobs ahead. Envision yourself doing the work before you actually start. By playing out these scenarios in your head, you might be amazed at how you discover methods to protect uninvolved areas of your home from becoming saturated with dust, and how well-prepared you are for the next day's projects. This is especially important when you have helpers and must have all building materials on site for them to begin work.

# Utilities & lighting

## CHAPTER 4

RELOCATING A WASHING MACHINE and clothes dryer from a garage or basement into a new laundry room and sewing center requires plumbing and electrical work. Your new office might even benefit from a small sink; utility rooms are great spots for deep sinks.

Along with pipes and wires, hollow areas between wall studs are commonly used to house other utility materials such as central vacuum system pipes, telephone wires, speaker wire, and the like.

Proper illumination of all work areas is a very important concern. Lack of sufficient light could be dangerous, especially when power tools are in use. Meager lighting causes workers to strain their eyes to clearly see what they are working on. Likewise, too much light or improperly positioned light fixtures could result in problems relating to glare and bright reflections that actually reduce vision ability.

Too much light is most often a problem near computer centers. Light reflected off a computer screen makes the electronic data almost impossible to read. Office and workspace lighting has become quite an issue of debate lately. Light fixture manufacturers and retail lighting companies have diligently studied the effects of illumination, and their advice to the consumer is invaluable. They suggest ideal lighting fixtures, the necessary amount, and the best physical positioning for your specific applications.

## Washing machines & clothes dryers

Just like any lavatory, the plumbing for washing machines requires hot and cold running water, plus a drain. Lavatory and washing machine plumbing differs, though, in the physical location of the pipes and the way the drain pipe exits walls.

Hot and cold water valves generally rest above a plastic drain pipe. The standard receptacle is supplied power by its own 20-amp circuit, dedicated to the washer (which means that no

other receptacles or light fixtures obtain power from it). Also needed is a 220-volt receptacle for the clothes dryer—also fed by a separate circuit.

Many homeowners find pipes and valves poking out from walls unsightly; they prefer to enclose them in plastic housings. A unit like this generally costs less than $10 and is very simple to install. Water valves and drain pipes are commonly located at or above the tops of washing machines, which simplifies connecting the machines' supply hoses.

Drain-pipe openings must be located higher than a washing machine's maximum water level, generally from about 36 to no more than 48 inches from the floor. Drain pipes must be no smaller than 1½ inches in diameter. Washing machine drain hoses should not fit tightly inside drain pipes, or water might be inadvertently siphoned from the machine during operation.

A P-trap is simply a bow in the drain pipe that actually traps and holds water, preventing sewer gas from filtering through drains and into living areas. Normally, washing machine P-traps are located at the bottom of vertical standpipes. This illustration shows the P-trap located just to the left of the standpipe, in order to avoid a stud.

Examine the photo on page 38. On the far left is a main drain that serves a kitchen sink above. The 2-inch drain pipe for this washer and utility sink will tie into it. To the right, a drain pipe has been run to a utility sink site. A vertical vent pipe will extend from the sink drain and tie into an existing vent line located about 10 feet away, above a lavatory. The installation of that vent pipe required the removal of drywall from the ceiling space above the bathroom.

Copper 1-inch pipe is commonly used to bring fresh water into residences. Inside the house, ¾-inch pipes run throughout walls and floor spaces toward sinks, tubs, and other destinations. The ¾-inch pipes give way to ½-inch pipes, which go directly to each accessory's faucet fixture.

The T's, elbows, and other fittings are soldered to copper pipe through a simple process. First, clean pipe ends and the inner openings of fittings with emery cloth. This step is important. The pipe and fittings should shine brightly. Then, apply a coat of flux to pipe ends and fitting interiors with a small brush. (Flux is a wax-like material that allows solder to firmly attach to copper pipe.)

Place the fitting on the pipe; heat with a propane torch. Do not aim the torch flame at the pipe—only at the fitting. Once the fitting and pipe have reached a perfect temperature, touch solder to the joint. Solder will instantly melt and be sucked into the cavity between the pipe and fitting. About ½ inch of solder is needed for ½-inch pipe connections, ¾ inch for ¾-inch pipe, and so on. If solder begins to drip off the fittings, you've used too much.

Threaded copper fittings are also soldered onto pipe. For inside threaded fittings, be sure fittings rest above the pipe while soldering. This prevents solder from flowing down onto threads and obstructing their grooves. Make threaded pipe connections by wrapping male threads with Teflon tape or another compatible sealer.

The plumbing for this washing machine and utility sink has been completed. Notice the pipe extensions sticking up from the copper water pipe outlet nipples; these vertical extensions serve as water-hammer dampeners. Air trapped inside them

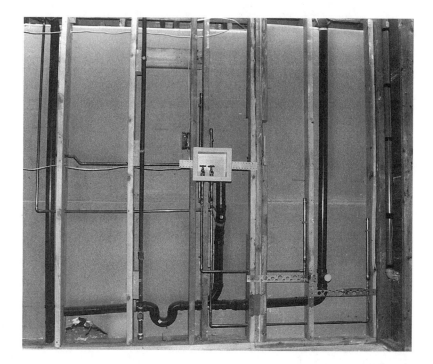

will compress and help slow down the flow of water when the flow is suddenly stopped, which can occur when a washing machine valve switches off or someone turns off a faucet quickly. Dampeners are about 12 inches long and made from ¾-inch copper pipe, and each is equipped with a cap, soldered on top. All pipes have been secured to studs with appropriate anchors or straps. Nailing plates cover pipe sections that are located closer than 1½ inch to stud faces.

Natural gas clothes dryers must receive gas from their own supply pipe. For the most part, ¾-inch black pipe is sufficient in size for runs up to about 80 feet. Black pipe connections are all threaded and never soldered. Coat the male threads with a sealer specifically designed for natural gas applications. Be certain connections are tight. Black ½-inch pipe runs from ¾-inch lines and to fixtures.

New natural gas line installations require a permit from the local building department. A building inspector will have to witness an air pressure test of the piping. This test is done by attaching an air pressure gauge to the pipe and filling it with about 15 psi; the system must hold that pressure for 10 to 15 minutes. Once the gauge has been disconnected, make the necessary pipe connections, turn on the gas, and test the new connections with a sudsy solution of liquid soap and water. Leaks will become clearly evident as soap suds begin to bubble.

Clothes dryers must exhaust to the outside. Flexible metal tubes of 4-inch diameter are available for this job, as are vents with hinged doors that secure to the exterior walls. Dryer exhaust hoses may only run up to about 25 feet. Each elbow in the line will reduce overall runs by 5 feet. Two elbows in an exhaust line, therefore, will reduce a maximum run to 15 feet.

Central heating systems supply heated air to rooms through ducts. These are generally 6-inch-diameter thin metal pipes that run between floor joists or in attic spaces. Sections are cut out of pipes for register installations.

## Heat ducts

This is an area directly above the featured washer and dryer installation. On the far right is a ¾-inch natural gas pipe. To the left of it, just before the heat duct, is a central vacuum pipe. Notice that it connects to a main line T at the bottom of the photo. The black-colored pipe running from left to right across the bottom of the photo is a drain for the kitchen sink above.

Make connections in heat duct materials by cutting flaps on ends of units that will be attached to main duct lines. The flaps are then bent over in opposite directions so that every other one will go inside the main duct and their counterparts will rest on the outside of the main duct.

Once the connection is inserted into the main duct, the flaps are squeezed against the main duct and then sealed with duct tape. Be sure to wear leather gloves while working with duct materials; the edges are very sharp.

## Electrical

Turn off the electricity at the circuit breaker or fusebox before working on outlets, switches, or any other electrical devices. Major alterations should be made by qualified electricians to ensure that everything is installed properly, according to the National Electrical Code.

It is a good idea to relocate an electrical receptacle from floor level to a site just above a countertop. How else will you be able to plug anything in once a counter has been installed over the lower outlet? First, turn off the circuit breaker that supplies power to the outlet. Then, using a new outlet box as a guide, trace around it with a pencil to designate where the new box will be installed. Cut away the wall with a drywall or keyhole saw, and attach the new box to the stud with screws from inside the box.

Run a comparable size wire, 14/2 or 12/2, from the old outlet to the new, and wire the receptacle. Connect the new black wire to the old black wire, white to white, and ground to ground with heavy-duty wire nuts in the old box. Cover the old box with a solid plate, and the new one with its receptacle cover. Turn on the circuit breaker and check the outlet with a tester to verify that it is operating properly.

This illustration depicts where a journeyman electrician is installing a new 200-amp circuit breaker panel. Notice that a portable light sits in the foreground. It was plugged into a heavy-duty extension cord which stretched to a neighbor's house; all electricity had been shut off during the circuit breaker panel installation.

Adding a new laundry room, renovating an old basement into a sewing and craft center, or turning an unused attic into a new office space entails running new electrical circuits. In some cases, the existing circuit breaker panels might be full. Only qualified electricians should install new panels.

This is a vacated bedroom that will soon be a modern laundry/sewing center. Initially, it was wired for only 15 amps of electricity. In addition, the room had no overhead lights. Two outlets were installed so that a lightswitch would operate their top plugs to activate lamps plugged into them.

In order to install a new circuit for the sewing center, the old receptacles were replaced with new models, and wiring was installed for recessed ceiling lights. Sections of drywall were removed to make the electrical wiring job a lot simpler and more efficient.

The electrical wire coiled at the top of this vertical opening will serve a NuTone Ironing Center. When planning to run wire for various appliances, pieces of equipment, or work centers, be certain to calculate how much electricity will be needed by all of your devices. Circuits are designed to flow 80% of their capacity at any given time. For example, a standard 20-amp circuit should never be required to supply more than 16 amps of power.

All electrical devices carry labels that designate how many amps they will draw. In some cases they might state this in watts, like 1500 watts for a hair blowdryer. Watts are divided by volts (120 volts for households) to come up with amps—1500 watts divided by 120 volts equals 12.5 amps. Therefore, calculate the amount of amps you will need for your new work center at any given time and be certain to supply that area with sufficient circuits.

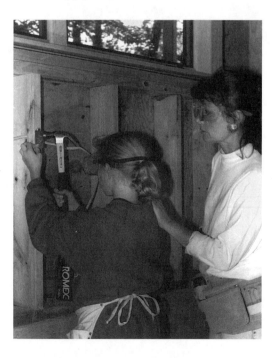

Wires that run through holes cut in studs or plates closer than 1½ inch to the face of the stud or plate must be protected with a nailing plate. These plates are equipped with pointed ears that allow them to be secured to studs with just a few hammer taps. Nailing plates prevent drywall nails or screws from coming in contact with wires.(See on previous page.)

Both of these receptacles are served by the same circuit. They will supply power to a sewing machine and serger. Although a single receptacle might suffice, two are installed to provide additional plugs for a radio or other small electrical device. Receptacles feature brass screws on one side and silver-colored screws on the other. Black wires are always secured to brass screws and white wires to the silver screws. Two jumper wires run from one receptacle to the other to supply it with power.

Once you have completed your electrical work, test receptacles to ensure that they are wired correctly. This handy tester features three lights. A label on top of the tester deciphers what it means when any combination of lights are lit or remain off. In this case, the center and right side indicators are lit. The left side is off, to designate that the receptacle is wired correctly.

## Lighting

Discuss your home office, work, and utility space lighting needs with a professional representative from a lighting store. He or she will be of great assistance in helping you determine which lights will best suit your work center needs and general decor preferences.

Power Products Company (SIMKAR) offers a host of different fluorescent light fixtures in a wide array of styles and sizes. This is a 4-foot, 4-bulb unit. Black, white, and ground wires connect to identical wires located inside electrical ceiling boxes. This housing will be secured to ceiling joists with screws or supported from ceiling drywall with toggle bolts. Instructions that accompany light fixtures are generally easy to follow.

This brand of anchor features a spring-loaded wing that is folded together to fit through a hole made in drywall. Once it passes through the hole, the wings flair out to rest on the inner surface of the drywall to support an object attached to it.

Fluorescent lights provide a greater amount of dispersed light than incandescent bulbs. They require a lot less electricity, too.

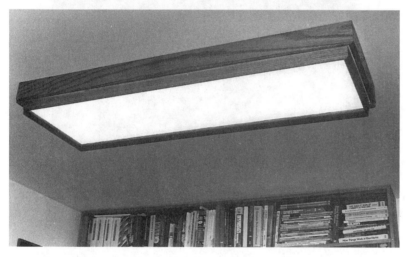

They are ideal for illuminating large spaces. For close-up work, like electronic hobbies, sewing, and other activities, supplement fluorescent lighting with incandescent bulbs operated from swing-arm lamps like those frequently seen on drafting tables.

Banks of fluorescent lights (on next page) are being installed in the second floor joist area of a new workshop. The 16 fixtures, each with 4 bulbs that are 4 feet long, will do an excellent job of supplying bright illumination to over 600 square feet. A string was stretched tightly from one end of the shop to the other and

used as a guide along light fixture ends to verify that they were installed straight in a row. This fixture style fits into joist areas, so that the faces are flush with the ceiling drywall.

**Recessed ceiling lights**

Recessed ceiling lights have become very popular. They are attractive, efficient, and inconspicuous. Many different housing and trim styles are available, each with specific application requirements. Trim units are designed only for certain compatible housings and vice versa. In addition, each housing and trim set will list the recommended types of light bulbs and wattages that can safely be installed in them.

For maximum effect, consider using dimmer switches for recessed ceiling lights. This could be perfect for office areas when computers are in use for extended periods of time.

48   *Home office, work, and utility spaces*

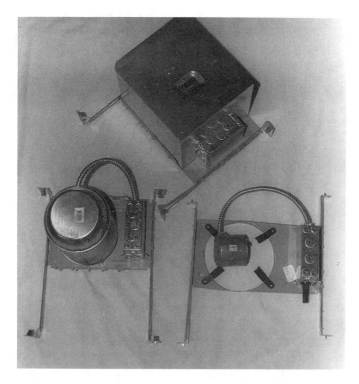

These are three types of recessed ceiling light housings from Halo. The one on the top is energy efficient; it is designed to allow insulation to come in contact with it, with no risk of fire. The model at lower right is not made for insulation contact—it will be used in a first-floor laundry/sewing center where there is no insulation in the ceiling/floor joist space. Recessed ceiling lights feature arms that extend out to span distances between joists. Tangs on their ends are simply nailed into joists.

R-30 insulation surrounds this energy-efficient recessed ceiling light. The light's housing includes double walls. Even after the 75-watt light bulb had been on for hours, the outer light housing was cool to the touch.

Recessed ceiling lights usually illuminate an area 6 feet in diameter. Special trim sets are available to focus light onto certain areas. Wall washers, for example, direct light toward walls to highlight paintings, bookcases, and other wall-mounted items.

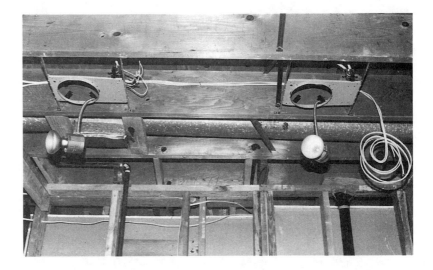

If you plan to install a number of recessed ceiling lights that operate from one switch, be certain the models you select are designed to be wired in series. These are just two of five lights installed in a new laundry/sewing center. All of them are wired together so they will operate off of a single lightswitch. No insulation is necessary for this ceiling/floor joist space, hence the use of this style of housing.

After the drywall was installed, finished, primed, and painted, the bulbs were removed for the installation of the light trim. This style simply calls for trim to snap onto the base. The trim is secured by four metal tangs that protrude from the housing frame. The open wall area to the right will support a built-in ironing center.

An excellent way to illuminate counter and desk areas is with under-cabinet fluorescent lights. Units mount directly to the bottom portions of cabinets above the countertop. Run a small section of wire from the electrical box to a hole in the wall just below a cupboard. Use the wire to pull a new section of electrical wire from the box to the under-cabinet light unit. A section of flexible conduit will protect the wire as it runs from the hole in the wall to the light unit.

There is no better time to install a central vacuum system than while walls are opened up for other utility work. Central vacuum systems incorporate a series of plastic pipe and fittings that run from different home areas down to a heavy-duty vacuum motor. Hoses range in length from 25 to 32 feet, so be sure you locate outlets in positions where hoses can reach into far corners and other out-of-the-way-spaces.

This central vacuum system runs off of regular 120-volt household electrical current. An inlet pipe attaches to a rubber connection mounted in the center of the unit's body. The pipe extending horizontally out from the unit's top section is an exhaust. A muffler is in place to keep noise at a minimum. The exhaust line will exit through an exterior wall to the outside.

A central vacuum pipe extends down from a second floor joist area to an outlet mounted in the wall about 18 inches from the

## Central vacuum system

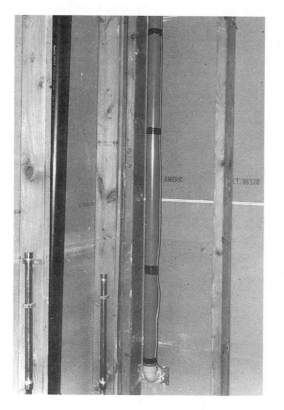

floor. An electrical wire is secured to the pipe with electrical tape. This wire supplies power to the outlet, so that when a flexible vacuum hose is plugged into it, the vacuum machine will automatically turn on.

Central vacuum system outlets are outfitted with spring-loaded doors equipped with gaskets. These doors prevent the loss of suction power while another outlet is being used.

Installing a central vacuum system is easy. The only hard part is deciding where to locate outlets and then actually installing pipe. Some drywall will have to be removed. Many installers cut drywall out from inside closets and other spaces, so that repairs made later remain out of sight.

## Summary

If you have never worked with copper plumbing pipe before, buy a section of pipe, some fittings, solder, flux, emery cloth, and a torch. Then practice. It shouldn't take you more than a few minutes to recognize how easy it is to solder pipes and fittings together. Likewise, understand that black ABS plastic pipe used for drains must be connected with glue especially designed for ABS pipe. Labels on cans of glue will plainly state that they are designed for ABS.

Electricity provides wonderful services, but it can also create catastrophes when handled inappropriately. If you have no experience working with electrical components, seek the assistance of a qualified electrician.

Finally, consult a lighting expert before you run out and purchase a bunch of new light fixtures. There are a number of different methods for calculating how much illumination is required for specific room sizes and the activities that will take place in them. Take advantage of an expert's experience so that your new home office, work, and utility spaces are illuminated for maximum benefit.

# Covering walls & floors

## CHAPTER 5

WOOD-FRAMED HOUSE WALLS are usually covered with drywall. There are exceptions, of course, especially in older homes that feature walls covered with lath and plaster. Because drywall is so simple to install, many do-it-yourself homeowners cover plaster walls completely with drywall instead of attempting plaster repairs. Drywall is simply placed over plaster and then secured to studs or joists with long drywall screws.

Hardwood floors are beautiful. Materials are available in kit form with boards already sealed and stained in a plethora of colors. Hardwood floor boards are nailed into position with a special nailing machine that can be obtained from a local rental store. Other floors are covered with sheet vinyl, carpet, tile, or vinyl squares. Shop around at home improvement centers and floor covering stores to find the best bargains and the most appealing products.

Drywall sheets are available in 4-foot widths and 8- to 12-foot lengths. The 4-x-8 size is employed most commonly. Drywall of ½-inch thickness is used for walls everywhere in the house, except between garages and living spaces. Those must be covered with ⅝-inch drywall. Although many drywall contractors install ½-inch drywall on ceilings, you might find better results using ⅝-inch material. This thickness of drywall will not sag between ceiling joists as much as ½-inch material.

The easiest way to install drywall is to hire someone to do it for you. In lieu of that, try the PanelLift Drywall Lift shown on next page. This piece of equipment can handle any drywall size. It will hold panels solidly against ceilings and upper walls while you insert drywall screws. Units are available for purchase or rental.

## Drywall installation

54   Home office, work, and utility spaces

Drywall must be placed against a solid backing, such as studs, joists, or plates. For remodelers, this can sometimes pose problems. On page 54, a section of drywall was removed for the installation of a recessed ceiling light. Since there were no blocks between joists at this point, a nailer was installed. (Nailers are nothing more than pieces of 2 × 4 nailed or screwed into a position along the edge of drywall to serve as a support.)

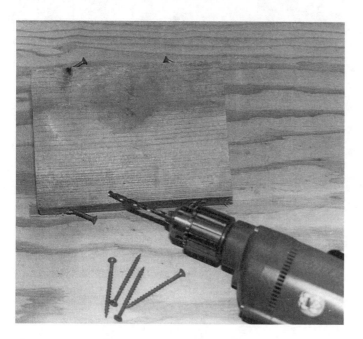

Holes were drilled at an angle through all four corners of this piece of 2 × 6. Long screws will be inserted into the holes and then driven into studs on each side to serve as a backing plate for a piece of drywall. (An angle drill/driver makes this job a snap.) Using this method of securing nailers is much easier than fighting with nails that must be toe-nailed, especially when you are working in awkward positions.

A long, metal nailing plate protects an ABS plastic drain pipe that rests closer than 1½ inch to the face of this stud. You can imagine how easy it might be to forget about that pipe while driving drywall screws into the next panel. Without nailing plates, you might not discover that screws have been driven into pipes until later, when you notice water damage from leaks. The metal plate above the nailing plate is a section of copper pipe support used to help secure ½-inch fresh water supply pipe nipples.

Cut drywall to fit around recessed ceiling lights, heat registers, wall switches, electrical receptacles, and anything else that protrudes out from walls. Place drywall sheets face up and take plenty of time to accurately transfer measurements taken along ceilings and walls onto drywall. Use a sharp razor knife to cut drywall.

For circles around recessed ceiling lights, try a drywall circle cutter from Stanley/Goldblatt. This tool will cut through the top layer of paper to denote an exact cutting line. Follow up with a razor knife or drywall cutting bit placed in a power trimmer. The metal T-square featured here is designed for drywall work and is very useful.

As hard as you try, measurements and drywall cutting might not always result in perfection. Expect to trim drywall edges a bit in order for them to fit around obstacles satisfactorily. Do not force drywall! Always use a sharp razor to trim it. Forcing drywall into place results in cracks, lumps, and other imperfections. Edges that were cut too far away from obstacles can be filled later with drywall compound and tape.

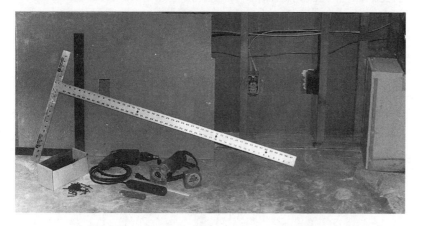

A section of drywall has been cut to fit into the open space to the right. Notice that a notch has been made at the piece's upper right corner. This was done so that a portion of the stud is exposed. A small square of drywall can be secured to it.

Drywall screws are easy to install with a drywall screwdriver. This tool adjusts to drive screws into drywall just far enough to create a small dent on the surface. Dents are later filled with drywall compound and sanded smooth to cover screws and make walls look perfect. Cuphead drywall nails may be used instead of screws. They must also be driven partially into drywall to make slight dents. Driving screws is a lot easier and much faster, than pounding nails.

Electrical receptacles were loosened and maneuvered so that holes in drywall could fit over them. Notice the small piece of drywall in the upper right corner of the new installation that fits into the notch made on the panel in the last illustration. Drywall screws are placed about 6 inches apart along studs.

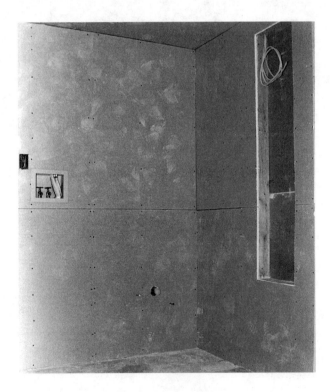

Drywall is typically installed horizontally on walls, with top panels positioned and secured first. On previous page, it was easier to install a solid piece of drywall along the top of the wall to the right and secure it with drywall screws than to cut it beforehand. After it was secured, a drywall saw was used to cut out a section for the ironing center. Afterward, the lower drywall panel was installed and secured. A section of this panel was also cut with a drywall saw using studs as cutting guides. Cutting drywall in this fashion was a lot easier and simpler than measuring and cutting the panels while they were on the floor.

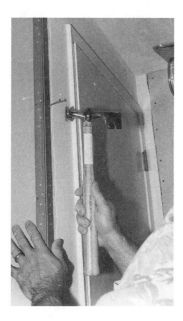

All outer drywall corners must be protected with corner bead. These metal strips are available at home improvement centers in 8-foot lengths. Simply cut them to length with a hacksaw and secure them with screws or nails. You do not have to sink screws or nails into dents while installing corner bead, as these strips are already formed at a slight angle to make room for drywall compound.

## Drywall finishing

Drywall compound, most often referred to by tradesmen as mud, comes in pre-mixed 1-gallon and 5-gallon containers or as a powder in bags. Mud is initially spread over all screws or nails, seams, joints, and other openings with a 6-inch drywall knife. Second mud applications are made with an 8-inch knife a day later, after the first coat has cured. It will be followed on the third day with a layer of mud applied with a 10- or 12-inch knife.

Along with the first coat of mud on seams, joints, inside corners, and other openings comes the application of drywall tape. Apply mud to a seam and then immediately put down a layer of tape. Use a bit more mud on your knife to firmly set tape into the initial mud application. Working with mud on inside corners is made a lot easier with the use of a special corner trowel that features two working sides.

Before applying a second coat of drywall mud, use a knife to scrape away and knock off hardened globs and imperfections. Since the second coat should result in a smoother surface, use 100-grit sandpaper and a sanding block to smooth imperfections before applying the third and final coat of drywall compound. Sanding the last coat of drywall compound to smooth perfection will create a tremendous amount of sanding dust. Seal off work areas from other rooms; wear safety goggles and a dust mask.

Another method for smoothing drywall compound, especially after the third and final coat, is referred to as wet sanding. This technique employs a large sponge dampened with water. Since compound is water soluble, a wet sponge acts swiftly to smooth the compound, leaving behind a flat and even texture. This method all but eliminates problems associated with sanding dust. Rinse sponges in clean water frequently.

Getting drywall joints and seams to an utterly smooth surface texture is exceptionally time-consuming and labor-intensive. This is why almost all drywall contractors apply a texture coat to entire walls and ceilings after work with compound is complete. Texture is usually applied with machines that can be rented from a tool rental yard. Machines are adjustable to create different types of texture. The material used in texturing is basically the same as drywall compound.

In lieu of renting a texturing machine, you might find satisfactory results applying a watered-down mixture of drywall compound with a thick nap paint roller. Follow each roller pass with a wide drywall knife to knock down compound to a suitable textured-surface appearance.

Applications of undercoat and semi-gloss enamel were achieved quickly with the Campbell Hausfeld HousePainter and

PaintPro Roller. Jobs were finished in about half the time it would have taken with a regular paint roller and pan. The PaintPro Roller kept paint splatter to an absolute minimum, and almost nonexistent.

Paint rollers cannot complete all painting tasks. Cut in with a brush in corners and on trim. Masking tape was used along this door jamb in the new laundry/sewing center to keep new paint off the old. Masking tape positioned accurately makes tight painting jobs much easier to accomplish. Be certain tape is pressed firmly onto surfaces to ensure that paint does not flow under open gaps.

## Window & door trim

Beautiful wood windows are highlighted by wood trim. Inexpensive metal windows that do not include inner window circumference trim may be finished with drywall. Cover corners with corner bead and finish like other drywall tasks. Wood trim outlining outer window openings is cut at 45-degree angles around all corners. Take your time while measuring, and use a chop saw with a sharp blade or a miter box for angle cuts.

This pneumatic brad nailer does an outstanding job of nailing trim in place. It is lightweight, maneuverable, and it countersinks nails. If you don't have a brad nailer, use small finishing nails and a nail set to drive nail heads below wood surfaces so holes can be filled with putty and sanded smooth.

Slight imperfections at trim corners must also be filled with putty and sanded smooth. Place nails into both wall studs and the wood edges of inner window trim. This way, outer trim can help keep inner trim in place and assist in preventing inner trim from bowing or buckling during extreme temperatures and humidity.

Victor Lopez, Technical Service Representative from the Behr Process Corporation, says that 95% of all paint and stain problems are related to users not following instructions listed on product labels. Pieces of clear wood, stained to perfection, are very attractive. They will remain that way for a long time when stain is applied correctly. Read labels and follow instructions. The directions should be concise and easy to understand.

## Floors

Use plenty of deck screws on subfloors and underlayment materials to keep floor squeaks at an absolute minimum. Imperfections on concrete floors must be corrected before floor coverings are installed to make walking surfaces feel smooth.

This portion of the new laundry/sewing center floor had a hump in it. A Makita Concrete Grinder made quick work of reducing that hump to a flat, even area. In place of the dust bag, a vacuum hose was taped in position over the planer's exhaust port and run over to the wet/dry vacuum. With the vacuum turned on, concrete dust was greatly eliminated from the planing operation.

Be certain to follow all operating instructions for concrete planers, paying strict attention to details regarding adjustments. This machine does an amazingly quick job of planing concrete. Incorrect adjustments will allow it to dig too deep into concrete surfaces, causing unnecessary imperfections.

Cracks and divots in concrete must be filled before vinyl floor coverings or carpet are installed. DAP's Latex-Fortified Cement Patch is available in both pre-mixed and dry forms. It dries fast, so only scoop out as much as you can use in a few minutes. Spread the patch with a trowel, being careful not to overfill depressions and leave behind lumps.

Floor vinyl is cut with a razor knife. It is easiest to write down floor dimensions on a piece of paper and cut vinyl out in a driveway or other open space. Cut the material an inch wider and longer all around to ensure you'll have plenty to work with inside your remodeled room. Then, roll up the vinyl, bring it into the work area, and unroll it carefully to avoid poking holes in it or causing creases.

Once vinyl is placed in position, use a razor knife to carefully cut around corners. Take your time and work slowly in order to achieve pleasing results. It is better to cut just a little, time after time, than to take a big chunk out and realize you goofed by cutting into the actual floor area.

Floor vinyl comes in rolls 12 feet wide. For rooms wider and longer than 12 feet, you will have to contend with seams. Lap one piece over the other and cut them at the same time to result in perfect seam joints. Then, apply vinyl seam glue to keep both edges attached securely together.

After you have successfully cut floor vinyl to size so that it fits perfectly (remember that baseboard molding will cover some minor flaws), roll half of the material back upon itself. Sweep the bare floor clean, and then apply floor vinyl glue according to label instructions. Different types of floor vinyl require different glue application procedures. Some simply require glue around perimeter edges, and others recommend specific sizes for the notches on trowel edges.

With glue applied, use a 100-pound floor roller to smooth vinyl and remove air bubbles. Rollers are available through floor-covering stores; many loan them out to customers free for a day. Using a roller is especially important for vinyl floors that require the entire floor to be covered with glue. If the material you install calls for use of a roller, then use one. If you don't, your incomplete job will result in hundreds of small lumps dotting the entire floor surface.

Carpeting is held in place with tack strips, small boards impregnated with hundreds of sharp tacks. Tack strips are nailed around floor perimeters about an inch or so away from walls. Padding is then rolled out and secured with staples.

Inexpensive carpet padding can make an expensive carpet feel thin and cheap. Do yourself a favor and install top-quality carpet pad for all of your carpet needs.

Cut large sections of carpet down to a manageable size out in a wide area, as recommended for vinyl. Once carpet is brought into the room, use a sharp carpet knife to cut around corners, obstacles, and along walls. You will need to rent a carpet stretcher in order to tightly secure carpet to tack strips. This simple device has teeth that grab hold of carpet as you kick a padded extension with your knee to stretch carpet. Use a wide-bladed carpet tool or putty knife to push carpet edges into place behind tack strip next to walls.

A special strip is used to secure carpet next to vinyl floors. Strips like this are available at home improvement centers. In doorways, cut carpet and pad directly under doors or at that part of the jamb where the door makes contact. The object here is to prevent one material or the other from being exposed on either side of doors while they are closed.

Use small nails to secure strips on wood floors and concrete nails on concrete floors. Because these nails are small, use needle-nose pliers to hold the nails while getting them started. On concrete, strike the nails good and hard so that they can be set with just one or two blows. If you try to tap concrete nails into position with repeated light blows, they will bend or chip out the concrete underneath them.

Once the strip has been secured to the floor, cut the carpet pad away from it (about 1 to 2 inches). Then, place the carpet edge firmly onto the strip and knock down the top bar with a block of wood and a hammer. Place the block of wood over the bar, then hit the wood block with the hammer. This should result in an even and dent-free evolution.

Fresh paint, wallpaper, a new floor covering, and other amenities are enhanced when smaller details are also updated or improved. Door knobs and handles are certainly one of those details.

## Other finishing ideas

Do the old, scratchy, and paint-covered door knobs and strike plates on your newly-remodeled office or workspace door look as good as the rest of your new area? Probably not. Seriously consider updating them with any of a number of handle, lever, or knob sets from Weiser Lock. Sets are packaged with complete installation instructions, including a template for designating exact areas where holes must be drilled into new doors. For new

exterior office and utility room doors, Weiser offers a number of attractive handle sets and dead-bolt locks.

After drilling holes for door handles, levers, or knobs, you will have to chisel out small sections of wood for strike plates and latches. Use a sharp pencil to outline their rectangular shapes, then employ a sharp chisel to carefully trim wood away inside the pencil lines. Continually check your work by fitting plates into the recesses after each second or third chisel pass. This patient endeavor will result in a perfect fit for the plates and an attractive installation.

A number of different devices are designed to keep doors from slamming into the walls behind them. Some incorporate a padded rod that screws into baseboard molding, and others are designed to hang from a door hinge. Here, a padded door-knob stop has been secured to the wall directly behind the knob. The stop came complete with an anchor and screw. Locating the right spot for the stop is easy; simply dab the knob with a felt pen and touch it to the wall.

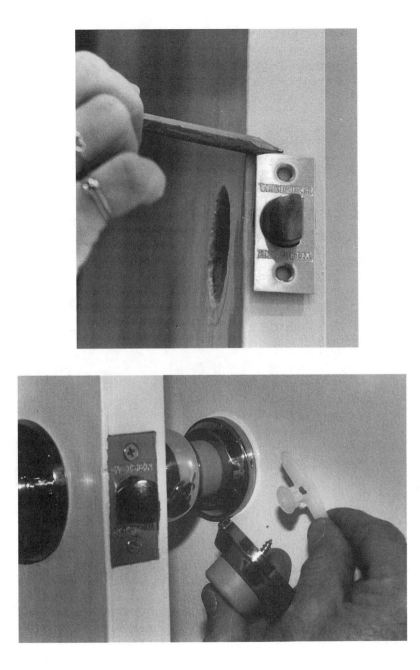

# Baseboard molding

A wide variety of wood and plastic base molding is available at home improvement centers, so select the style desired with your budget in mind. If you plan to paint the base molding, you might opt for less-expensive grades instead of clear, knot-free, solid-wood materials. See below for a quick picture of how to deal with molding.

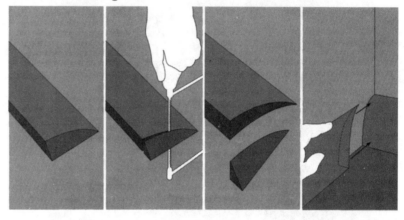

## CHAPTER 6

# Shelves, bookcases, & cupboards

Although shelves, bookcases, and cupboards are all used to store things up off of floors, each has its own design characteristics. Shelving units most frequently feature separate, open bases made of wood, glass, or other material supported by brackets of some kind. They might be made of lightweight materials for simply displaying curios and other small objects, or they could be made of sturdy metal, capable of holding hundreds of pounds.

Bookcases, for the most part, are envisioned as attractive units built out of thick wood, trimmed and stained to a rich hue, and filled with hardback encyclopedias and other comparable books. They must be constructed of heavy materials and solidly braced to support the amount of weight placed on them by volumes and volumes of heavy books.

Cupboards differ from the others in that they have doors. As with shelving units and bookcases, shelves must be made to hold up under the weight they are expected to support. Lightweight cupboards could never be expected to safely store large volumes of paint, but they might do an excellent job of keeping craft and sewing materials neatly tucked away, protected from sunlight and dust.

## Shelves

Utility shelving units are available in a variety of prefabricated materials. Particleboard units are plentiful and sold in boxes; buyers must put them together. Some models require nailing, others don't. Metal shelving systems, put together with nuts and bolts, are also available. Although they might lack eye appeal, units like these serve useful functions in basement hobby centers, garage workbench spaces, and similar home areas.

It took only a few minutes to assemble this plastic storage system. It features four shelves supported by 16 plastic tubes. Tubes may be cut to accommodate special shelf heights. Small holes located on lips at the rear of the shelves are intended for the insertion of screws that will secure units to walls.

Most folks regard brackets as things that support shelves from below. In this case, a bracket was mounted upside down over a window. Because of its design that includes an angular brace, this bracket supports a pine shelf from above very well in a work center area. A lip on the shelf helps to prevent spraypaint cans from falling. Since a solid-wood header is located directly above the window, there was little concern about finding a stud for securing the bracket.

Adjustable shelves are most convenient. They can be moved up or down to accommodate the size of things stored on them. In lieu of carefully measuring and marking each spot for a hole to be drilled for brackets, employ a piece of pegboard as a guide. Bracket pins like these are commonly sold at home improvement centers in a number of colors and styles.

Brackets that support shelves must be secured to wall studs for optimum strength. For lightweight applications in spaces where

studs might not fall within desired locations, use sturdy drywall anchors, and limit shelf storage to smaller, lightweight objects. Many brackets sold in packages will have label information regarding the maximum amount of weight they are capable of safely supporting.

## Basic bookcase/cupboard construction

As described earlier in the book, the main differences between many home storage units are in the types of materials used and the manner in which units are adorned with trim and molding. The following pages will cover one bookcase/cupboard project from beginning to end. Keep in mind that the use of different materials would have made this particular project look completely different, even if similar assembly methods were employed.

For a bookcase/cupboard designed to fit into a corner of a new laundry/sewing center, two separate units will be joined together at the corner. White Melamine is used for panels to brighten the interior storage area for maximum visibility. Solid oak rails and stiles will adorn the front to result in an attractive, sturdy configuration.

Melamine is a product that incorporates particleboard sandwiched between two layers of scratch-resistant material. It comes in 4-x-8 sheets in both ½- and ¾-inch thicknesses. Panels are available in white or almond colors. The ¾-inch-thick Melamine generally produces the best results. Be advised that this material is very heavy. Plan to have someone help you maneuver full sheets.

In lieu of a panel saw, the safest way to cut full sheets of Melamine or plywood is with a circular saw and guide. Place sheets on top of four 2 × 4s, with two boards on one side of a cut and two on the other. This way, both halves will remain equally supported during and after cutting tasks.

A metal guide bar with clamps was placed 15¹¹⁄₁₆ inches away from one Melamine edge. This distance accounted for the span between a Makita 7¼-inch circular saw blade and the saw's base plate edge that would rub against the guide. This resulted in panels that were cut at exactly 12 inches wide. Here, a Makita Slide Compound Saw with a new blade is used to cut a 12-inch-wide panel to length. Remember, sharp clean saw blades make a world of difference when you are cutting wood for finish carpentry projects.

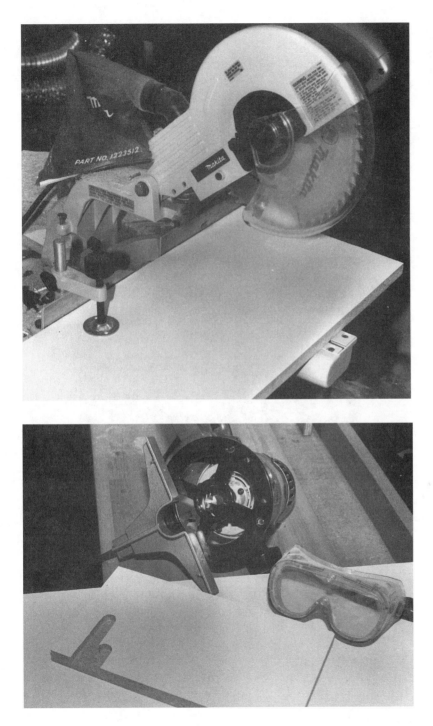

Melamine panels 12 inches wide will be used for cupboard floors, tops, shelves, and side panels. For maximum support, floor units will fit into dado grooves cut into side panels. A ¾-inch straight router bit is employed for this dado groove maneuver. The bit was carefully adjusted so it would cut to a depth of ⅜ inch; half the thickness of the ¾-inch Melamine panel. Making dado grooves half the thickness of supporting materials is relatively standard practice. Make test cuts on scrap material to ensure accurate router adjustments.

Routers must be used with guides. Most routers are equipped with guides for work near wood edges. Here, a dado groove has been made in the center of a cupboard end panel; the unit is resting on its back side. This groove will support one end of a fixed shelf running through the center of the unit. Notice that the board used for the router is clamped in place. An accurate measurement was taken between the edge of the router bit and edge of the router's base plate to determine where this board should be positioned.

The router work was completed successfully; the center shelf fits nicely into the groove. Wood glue was spread throughout the groove and drywall screws driven in through the end panel to keep the shelf secure.

A #8 countersink drill bit was used to drill pilot holes into the top of this unit to secure a vertical center support and divider. The drill bit made room for screws so they would not split the

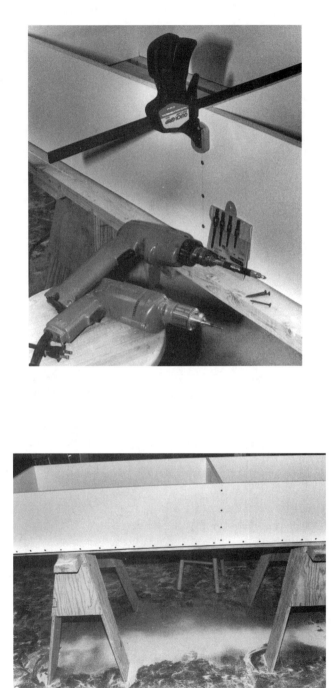

Shelves, bookcases, & cupboards    77

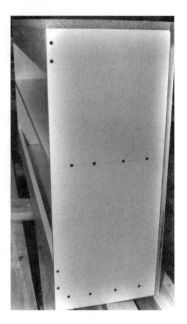

Melamine material when driven into it. In addition, this particular bit made a larger hole on the top surface. The screw heads fit perfectly in the indentation, resting flush with the surface. A pencil line was drawn down the center of the groove with assistance from a square. This line made it easy to determine where pilot holes should be drilled and screws driven.

On previous page, a number of screws were driven through the bottom of this unit to secure it to a cleat, located directly above. That cleat will be secured to wall studs with larger, #8 3-inch-long screws. Another means to secure cupboard floor sections is to cover the back sides of units with a piece of comparable ¾-inch material. Back panels would be cut to the same dimension as side panels so that a section could extend past the floor. A groove would be routed or dadoed along the lower section of the back panel in line with the groove on end panels so that the floor of the cupboard could also fit into it and be secured with screws from behind and out of sight.

With the cupboard/bookcase standing upright, you can see two cleats: one just below the top shelf and one just above the bottom floor. Notice that screws securing the three shelves and the two cleats are clearly visible on this end panel. That is of no concern at this end; it will be placed out of sight up against another corner unit. The other end panel will be covered with real wood veneer to completely change its appearance. Since a countersink drill bit allows screws to rest flush with the surface, veneer will go on neat and smooth.

After Melamine has been cut, a bare particleboard surface will remain. This is not a concern for edges that will rest against walls or panels, but must be accounted for on edges that will face forward or otherwise remain visible. Bare edges are easy to cover with Melamine edging material. Rolls of edging are a bit wider than ¾ inch and come in lengths up to 50 feet.

Simply adjust a regular clothes iron to its cotton setting and apply it to the edging. Heat from the iron will melt edging glue and firmly affix it in place. Use a sharp razor knife to trim excess edging, and a sandpaper and block to gently remove other small irregularities. Be advised that the pungent fumes from the melting glue will rise above work pieces and make your eyes water. Keep your head tilted back.

On the next page, the basic frame for this unit has been completed. Cleats and a center panel support should keep both the top and bottom shelves secure, especially when screws are driven through both cleats and into studs 16 inches on center. Now, work begins to transform this ordinary utility grade unit into something much more eye appealing—the installation of solid oak rails and stiles that measure ¾ inch thick and 2 inches wide.

Rails and stiles are attached directly to units with finishing nails that are covered with putty and sanded smooth. Rails and stiles are secured to each other in two different fashions. One method employs a small metal block that features a hole drilled through it at an angle. This block is clamped to the back of a board and used as a guide for drilling pilot and screw access holes. Screws are inserted through the holes at an acute angle and into intersecting rail or stile members.

Another method employs the use of a biscuit cutter and wood biscuits, or splines. First, this vertical stile was placed against its horizontal rail counterpart in a precise position. A pencil line was drawn across the joint in the middle of the stile and onto the rail. The biscuit cutter was accurately adjusted to cut in the center of the ¾-inch-thick boards, only deep enough for a small #0 biscuit. The pencil lines were used as guides for the cutter. With cuts made on both pieces, grooves and the biscuit were saturated with wood glue.

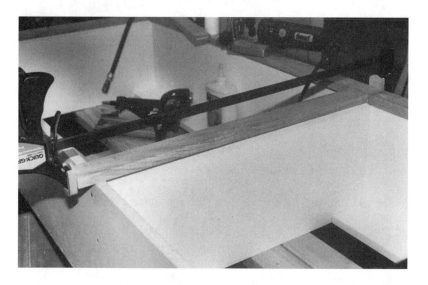

With the biscuit inserted into the rail's groove, the stile's groove was positioned around the biscuit and next to the rail. A clamp is now holding the pieces firmly together. Since the rail has already been secured to the cupboard unit, this stile will be nailed to the center Melamine support and shelf with finishing nails.

This unit is nearly ready to be hung on a new laundry/sewing center wall. Notice that thin strips of oak were glued and nailed to shelf edges. An area to the right has no rail or stile members. This is because another unit will be mated to it at that point. All that's left to do is to set the finishing nails and sand the face with #100 and then #240 sandpaper attached to an orbital or finishing sander.

Fill nail holes and minor gaps between rails and stiles easily with a dab of wood glue. Wipe off excess and then sand the area thoroughly. Sanding dust will attach to the glue and fill holes with actual material right from the wood itself.

Asking a couple of helpers to hold a heavy cupboard unit in place while you drill pilot holes and drive screws is a bit much, especially for heavy units made out of ¾-inch material. A better solution is to drive 16d nails into studs at approximate heights where the bottoms of the cleats will rest.

Determine where you want the tops of units to be in relation to the ceiling, and then measure the distance from the tops of the units to the bottoms of the cleats. Add those measurements together and drive nails into studs at those points, as measured from the ceiling. Once nails have been driven into studs, have a helper assist you in gently placing units on them. Have that helper brace up one end or the other until the units are perfectly level. Drill pilot holes through cleats; sink #8 3-inch screws through them and into studs.

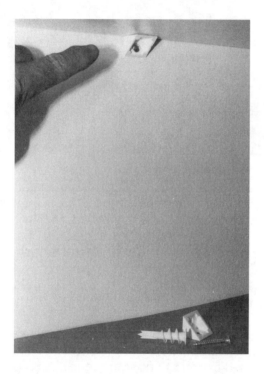

The unit with a fixed center shelf has been secured to the wall with #8 3-inch screws placed 16 inches on center and driven into studs. The front of the center shelf is supported by a stile. Here, an angle bracket has been secured to the wall with a heavy-duty anchor. This bracket will support the rear edge of that center shelf. The drywall anchor featured here is simply screwed into drywall with a Phillips-head screwdriver. Its sharp point makes its own hole, and wide threads keep the fastener firmly in place.

Both cupboard/bookcase units have now been installed. Notice a very slight gap along the stiles where both units meet. This was caused by an irregularity in the drywall at that corner of the room. A small piece of oak trim will hide that flaw. Holes drilled on the inside panels of the right hand unit were made for pin brackets that will support one or two extra shelves. The holes were made with a ¼-inch drill bit that was guided by a piece of ¼-inch pegboard.

The adjustable shelves are supported in the middle of their lengths by pin brackets inserted into vertical cleats. The shelves had to be notched in order to fit around the cleats. The notches were made about ⅛ inch wider and deeper than the cleats for easy maneuvering. Holes were drilled on the inside face of the center stile for the insertion of pin brackets. The 44-inch shelves are now supported at both ends and in the middle to prevent any problems with bowing.

For optimum protection against bowing shelf boards, plan to provide center support for shelves as follows: solid pine shelves—maximum of 36 inches on center; plywood shelves—

maximum of 30 inches on center; particleboard shelves—
maximum of 24 inches on center.

With regard to nail and screw sizes, the following guide might
be helpful: ¾-inch plywood—#8 screw, 6d case/8d finishing nail;
⅝-inch plywood—#8 screw, 6d case/8d finishing nail; ½-inch
plywood—#6 screw, 6d case/4d finishing nail; ⅜-inch plywood—
#6 screw, 4d case/3d finishing nail; ¼-inch plywood—#4 screw,
3d case/brads.

Older cabinets with main components still in excellent
condition can look like new with help from Quality Doors. The
company will manufacture custom-made cabinet doors and
drawer fronts to your specifications.

## Cabinet refacing

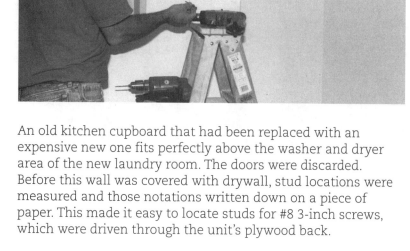

An old kitchen cupboard that had been replaced with an
expensive new one fits perfectly above the washer and dryer
area of the new laundry room. The doors were discarded.
Before this wall was covered with drywall, stud locations were
measured and those notations written down on a piece of
paper. This made it easy to locate studs for #8 3-inch screws,
which were driven through the unit's plywood back.

Undercoat was applied first, and then the interior of the unit was painted with a semi-gloss enamel. It now matches the Melamine units located across the room. The painted rails and stiles will be sanded smooth with #100 sandpaper and a sanding block. That will remove uneven surface textures around old hinge points and along the top where a piece of painted trim had been located.

Strips of real wood veneer will be cut from a 24-x-96-inch roll. Strips will measure slightly longer and wider than the rails and stiles. They will be attached to rails and stiles by the removal of a paper backing to expose their adhesive. After veneer is pressed into position with the veneer tool, use a sharp razor knife to cut off excess. A Quality Doors video tape explains the entire cabinet refacing process in detail.

Real wood veneer is used on this new unit to cover a Melamine end panel. Half of the veneer is in place on the left, next to an end stile. That edge was positioned first and perfectly in line with the stile, since trim would not look good at that location. Paper is slowly pulled from the back of the veneer piece to maneuver it carefully into position.

With solid oak rails and stiles, and real wood veneer on the end panels, this unit is starting to look nice.

The brad nailer is used to quickly secure a piece of oak trim to the corner of this end panel where it meets the wall.

Had these units been constructed out of hardwood plywood instead of Melamine, they could remain open and serve as

attractive bookcases. As it is, they will be equipped with doors to serve as cupboards that hold an array of sewing and craft materials.

Quality Doors (shown on previous page) are available in a number of different styles: from solid oak models to of laminate. These doors were ordered for other projects that required different sizes. Remember, Quality Doors builds custom-made units to the exact specifications you provide. They can build any door or drawer front to fit any cabinet—new or old.

## Additional ideas

In hobby rooms, workshops, craft centers, and even utility rooms, extra storage space might be provided by small sections of pegboard attached to the backs of solid doors. Pegboard must rest away from the door surface a minimum of ¼ inch to allow room for the insertion of the pegs. This hobby workbench was made from ¾-inch ACX plywood and trimmed with strips of pine to cover plywood edges.

To separate two different home work areas, consider installing a bookcase/divider. Such a unit could lend an air of privacy between work centers, and also provide additional storage.

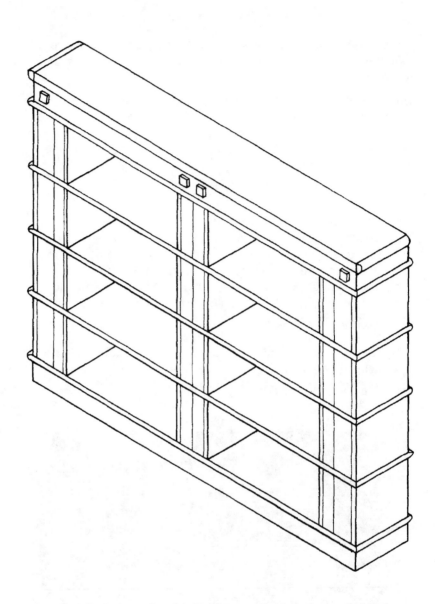

More detailed plans for this bookcase/divider are available from
Western Wood Products Association

# Office accommodations

## CHAPTER 7

An office design for one person might not suit the needs of another. Although office jobs generally entail paperwork, people have different needs with regard to files, bookcases, desks, open worktops, drafting tables, and so on.

A researcher will need lots of room to store reference materials. A person in the graphic arts business might prefer wide working tables that tilt and are equipped with adjustable arm lamps. You have to decide which accommodations will best suit your needs.

Experts in the field of ergonomics recommend various dimensions for office equipment and work centers. For example, some suggest that computer screens should be located around 20 degrees below an operator's line of sight and from about 1 foot to 1½ feet away his or her eyes. Most desk heights range from 29 inches to 30½ inches, but some experts feel that 28 to 28½ inches is much more comfortable. Typewriter and computer keyboard heights should be lower, from about 23 to 25 inches.

Spend time sitting at different desks at office supply stores to see which one fits you the best—then measure it. Build your own work center to the dimensions that suit you most comfortably and outfit it with the types of storage and conveniences you really want.

For those forced to complete office work at kitchen tables, a miniature office built out of a closet might be heaven sent. Others with growing home businesses might cherish thoughts of an office the size of a three-car garage. Of course, we are all forced to live within our means and the space available to us in our homes. Take advantage of what you have, and aspire to turn those spaces into super-functional, efficient, and comfortable workspaces.

## Floor plan ideas

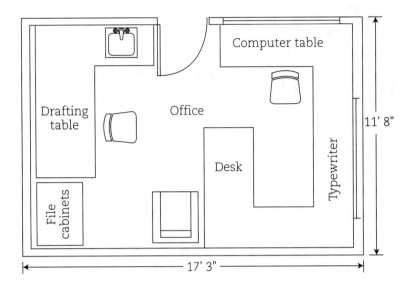

An office this size is quite large for most homes, unless you are lucky enough to have a house that features a large open attic area or viable basement space. A U-shaped work area will provide lots of desktop working space and plenty of room for shelves, cupboards, or bookcases above.

This setup would accommodate the efforts of two people working in the office, with a third resting comfortably in an easy chair. Large drawers under work centers could be outfitted with two-drawer file cabinets for extra filing needs. The sink is a nice feature for making coffee or washing hands after spending a few hours at the drafting table.

Because many bedrooms measure 10 × 12 feet, this office design might work out great for some homes. The drafting table area could be located in what was once a clothes closet, and the computer table could be located under a window with a view. Use graph paper to draw out different floor plans, using two squares to the foot. Measure the desk and furniture items you already have and draw their dimensions into the plan. This

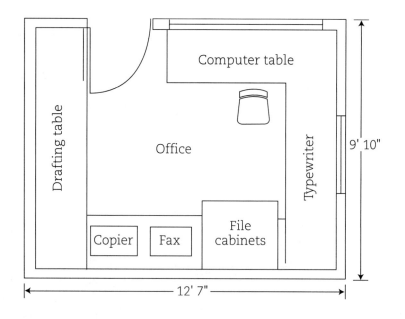

should help you get a good grasp of just how everything will fit into your new office area.

The set of plans starting on the next page is for an attic storage unit. It doubles as a viable office space.

Additional plans are available from the American Plywood Association, as well as from the Western Wood Products Association. The plans are inexpensive, generally well under $5.

Open spaces under stairways are often wasted on curio shelves or other things. A plan from the Western Wood Products Association can show you how to turn such a space into a functional desk area.

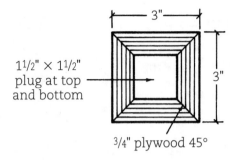

$1^1/_2" \times 1^1/_2"$
plug at top
and bottom

3"

3"

3/4" plywood 45°

**Fascia detail**

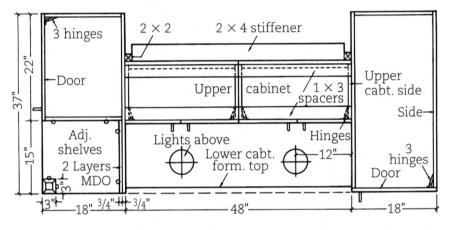

3 hinges

2 × 2

2 × 4 stiffener

22"

37"

Door

Upper | cabinet

1 × 3
spacers

Upper
cabt. side

Side

15"

Adj.
shelves

2 Layers
MDO

Lights above

Lower cabt.
form. top

Hinges

12"

3
hinges

Door

3"

3"

18"

3/4"

3/4"

48"

18"

**Top view**

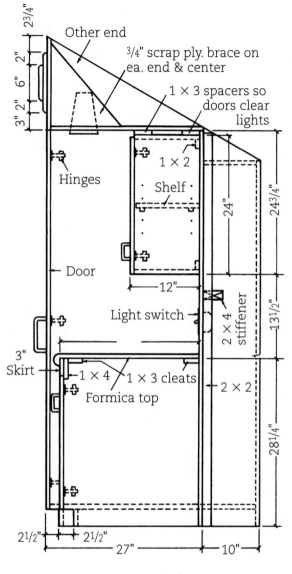

Other end

3/4" scrap ply. brace on ea. end & center

1 × 3 spacers so doors clear lights

23/4"

2"

6"

3" 2"

1 × 2

Shelf ·

Hinges

24"

243/4"

Door

12"

Light switch

2 × 4 stiffener

131/2"

3" Skirt

1 × 4    1 × 3 cleats

Formica top

2 × 2

281/4"

21/2"    21/2"

27"    10"

**Cross section**

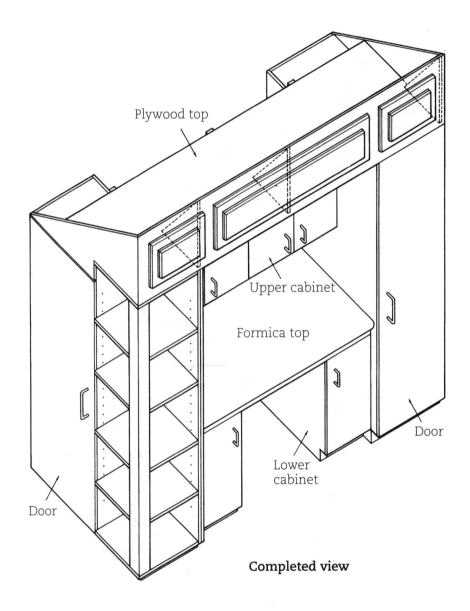

Plywood top

Upper cabinet

Formica top

Door

Lower
cabinet

Door

**Completed view**

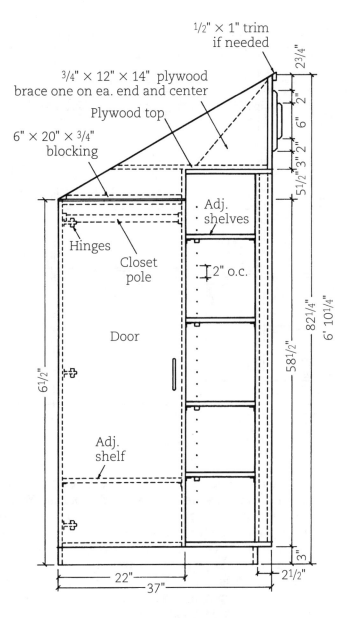

**Left end view**

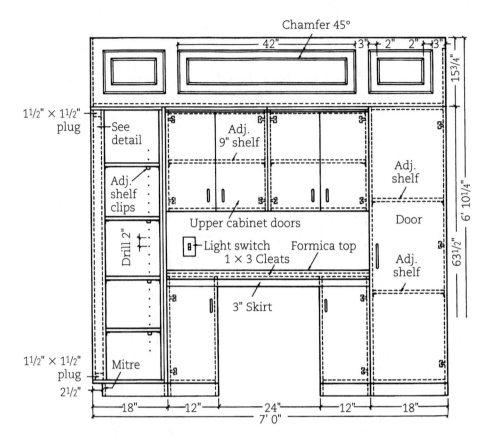

**Front view**

## Setting up desk areas

Building beautiful desks like the ones you see in fine furniture stores requires a great deal of time and expertise. You will have to amass a lot of knowledge about fine woodworking and furniture making before you tackle such projects. However, this does not mean you can't build a comfortable desk out of hardwood plywood and boards. Carefully inspect inexpensive particleboard desks at office supply stores to see how easy they are to assemble. Then, instead of particleboard, use a high grade of hardwood plywood to build your desk.

As you should notice at office supply stores, many desks are assembled with brackets, special clips, and other unique fasteners. You can employ the same fasteners; most are available at home improvement centers and woodworking supply stores. The round brackets located under a desktop secure a vertical panel located at the rear of the chair opening.

Hardwood plywood panels constitute two end panels attached to the horizontal member to make a basic frame. The top rests on these panels, and two other smaller panels provide support for drawers on both sides of the chair opening. Metal guides located on both sides of the center bracket support a computer keyboard tray or center drawer.

Drawers are easy to install, especially when Hafele bottom-mount roller guides are used. These units are rugged and glide smoothly with nylon rollers. A plastic bracket at the left of the guide is used to secure guides from rear desk panels. This deep drawer is perfect for files.

Hanging file folders do an excellent job of keeping files separated and organized. Metal frames are quick to assemble with just a screwdriver and pliers. They are available in letter and legal size. Use them to store manila folders that might be filled with important documents and correspondence. Before building base cabinets, filing cabinets, and other drawer units, be sure to purchase hanging file folder assemblies first, so that your drawers can be built to accommodate them.

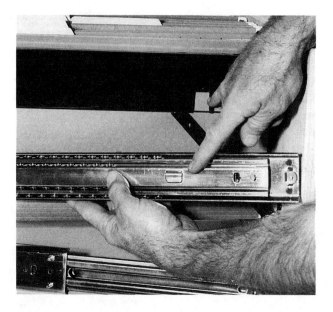

In lieu of actual drawers for hanging file folders, consider this arrangement. A metal frame is attached to a drawer front with screws. Two brackets extend down from the frame at an angle to the drawer front to add support. The frame hangs from two heavy-duty guides that are screwed to the sides of cabinets or desk openings. Hanging file folders rest on top of the frame to support manila folders and other materials.

New desks, file cabinets, cupboards, and other drawers or doors must be outfitted with handles or pulls as shown on last page. Take your time to select them, since specific design details could really add to the overall appearance of your desk and office area. These are just a few of the handles available from Häfele. All are made completely from solid wood, except for the one in the middle, which features brass ends.

A common problem that plagues home office laborers is wobbly desks and work centers. This dilemma could be caused by uneven work units or wavy floors. Solve those kinds of problems quickly and easily with adjustable feet or simple plastic wedges. These products are simple to install and adjust. The foot simply screws onto an inside desk corner, and plastic wedges are segregated into squares so that when enough has been positioned under desk legs, the excess is merely broken off. These are excellent items for desks that rest on top of carpet.

As mentioned earlier, ergonomics experts believe computer screens should be positioned at specific distances away from

and below users' eyes. This is not always easy to accomplish; many computers are designed for screens to rest on base units. This computer screen stand is fully adjustable; you can place screens at any elevation or angle desired.

To help open up working spaces on desk tops, check with your computer dealer to see if the base unit you have could be located on its side on the floor. This would get that piece of equipment out of your way to allow for more working space. The screen stand will help clear the desktop area even more.

The screen stand on the next page is designed to house cables inside a hollow area along its support arm. The space is covered to keep cables out of sight and away from work centers.

The unit on the next page also features a handy tray for computer keyboards. It is adjustable to accommodate almost any keyboard.

The most comfortable place to install a keyboard is below the level of the desktop. A variety of under-desk keyboard supports and trays are available.

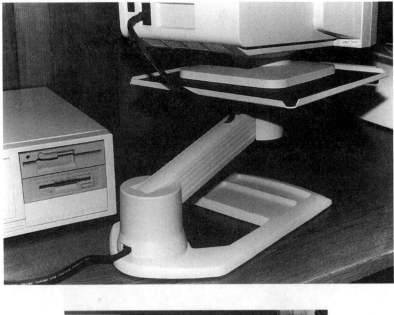

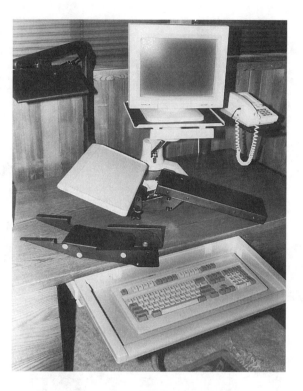

The unit on the bottom works off two guides attached to the underside of the desk. In the middle rests a unit that operates on swivels. The unit in back is a heavy-duty model that features adjustable knobs so users can find the most comfortable positions.

The cost of computer keyboard supports varies widely, and the most expensive are completely adjustable. If you spend hours and hours at a keyboard five or more days a week, treat yourself to the top of the line model. You will be more comfortable.

The keyboard tray on the next page comes with a template that shows exactly where to drill pilot holes for mounting screws. The template includes three sections for different desk applications. Make the installation easy by taping the template under the desktop before attempting to drill pilot holes.

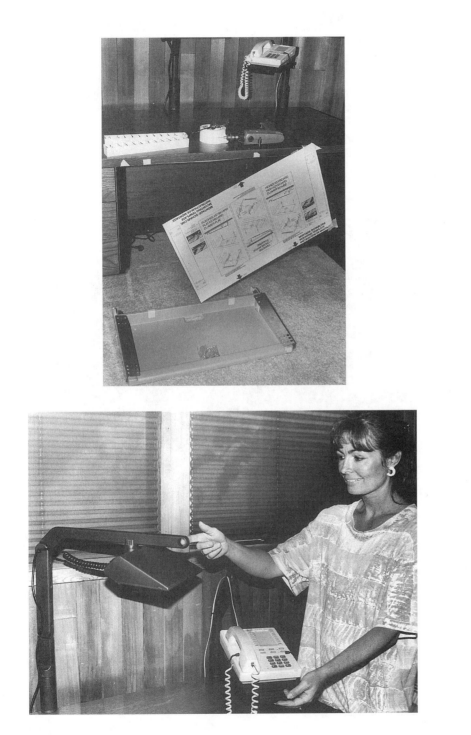

Sufficient illumination and clear work areas are two important home office concerns. The halogen desk lamp on page 107 is adjustable in all directions and can be mounted to desks with a clamp or by way of a base screwed to the desktop. These options allow you to place lamps virtually anywhere.

The telephone stand also on page 107 is excellent. It gets another piece of equipment off the desktop, and its arm conveniently locks in three different positions. Plastic clips on both units keep cords off desktops and out of the way.

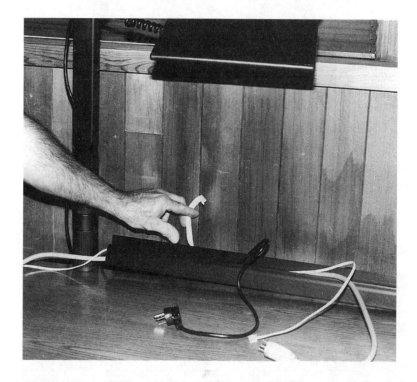

Modern office areas are filled with electrical cords, computer wires, and telephone lines. How many times have you had trouble with tangled wires scattered about your desktop? A simple and inexpensive solution is a Häfele cable trunk. Cable trunks are long pieces of plastic molded to hold cords and cables out of the way. They come in 10-foot lengths, easily cut with a hack saw. A strip of adhesive on the back holds them in position along walls.

This simple hardwood plywood desk offers a wide working surface and plenty of drawers for storing supplies and correspondence. A computer printer rests on its own stand just to the left. Ideally, this computer base unit could be stored on the floor, under the drawers on the left, to offer even more working room. A large drawer at bottom left is perfectly suited for files.

Frequently used floppy discs, stored in a wall-mounted rack, will free up drawer or desktop space for other things.

## Summary

Above all, home offices must be set up for the ultimate convenience of those who use them. No storage or floor plan idea is too crazy as long as the overall method of organization works well for you. Envision yourself working in your current office space to calculate how many wasted steps you take to retrieve materials on a frequent basis. How can you position and store those items within arm's reach?

Without a doubt, the most convenient and efficient home office would be one that allows you to reach everything you need without having to get up out of your chair. At the end of a workday, you would feel relaxed and totally at ease.

## CHAPTER 8

# Work & craft centers

Plan your new work center as carefully as you would a new office and its accessories. The type of center you design should suit the endeavors you will be pursuing there. Are you in need of a simple, organized arrangement for washing and drying clothes? Fold-out tables for periodic repair tasks? Mobile work stations? Contemplate exactly what type of work station is best for you, and then begin designing a facility that will meet those needs.

## Simple work areas

It has been said that simplicity is the mother of invention. Less eloquently, there's "K.I.S.S.—Keep It Simple, Stupid." Wise sayings or rude remarks? Either way, remember them as you plan.

At times, something as simple as a stool can make all the difference in the world for a project to proceed smoothly. A frequently used tool, hung from an accessible hook just above a work center, can save lots of time and aggravation. What do you plan to accomplish at your new work center? Which tools, implements, or devices do you need most often?

Stop, think, and envision yourself actually puttering around a work station. Recognize what actions you take consistently to accomplish regular tasks in the working conditions you have at present. Is there a better way? Could supplies and materials be located more conveniently? Would you be more comfortable working at a center that is raised higher or dropped to a lower position?

Pegboard panels located near work centers offer ideal spots for storing frequently used tools and other implements. Why store things in a drawer, forcing yourself to open it numerous times a day? Keep frequently used items stored clearly in view and readily accessible; your work efforts will be enhanced and your projects less stressful.

A simple workbench, outfitted with a lower shelf and made out of sturdy ¾-inch ACX plywood, is versatile. Gardening supplies could be stored within easy reach. Pieces of equipment for hobbies would be easy to retrieve, like scroll saws and disc/belt sanders. A wide worktop is ideal for numerous home improvement or crafts activities.

This workbench was assembled using corner brackets and screws. It was easy to make, and can be built to any height. Plans for workbenches similar to this are regularly available at lumber yards, home improvement centers, and other outlets.

For homes located in warm climates, where laundry centers are typically located in garages, the following set of plans might be just the answer to a cluttered laundry problem. For homes where cold winter months make clothes washing impossible in unheated garages, a simple set of upper cupboards with a folding table below might be just the ticket for keeping the utility room clutter-free.

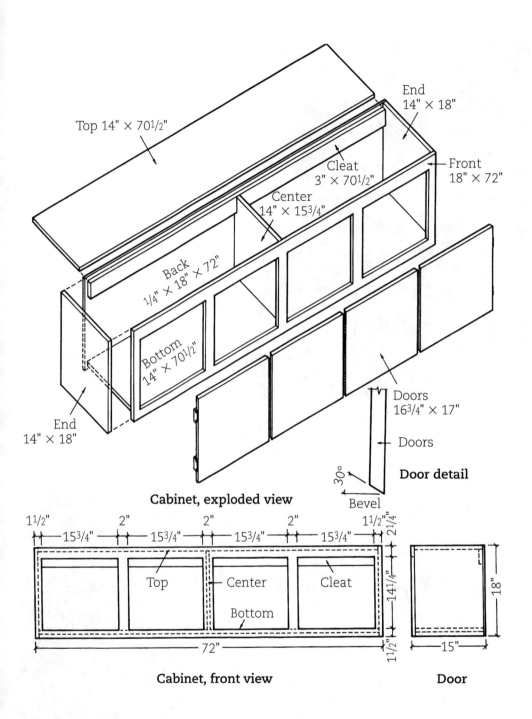

Top 14" × 70½"

End
14" × 18"

Cleat
3" × 70½"

Front
18" × 72"

Center
14" × 15¾"

Back
¼" × 18" × 72"

Bottom
14" × 70½"

End
14" × 18"

Doors
16¾" × 17"

Doors

Door detail

30°

Bevel

**Cabinet, exploded view**

1½"    2"        2"        2"      1½"    2¼"

15¾"    15¾"      15¾"      15¾"

Top    Center    Cleat      14¼"

Bottom    18"

1½"

72"    15"

**Cabinet, front view**    **Door**

Fold down work bench

24" × 42"

2 × 4

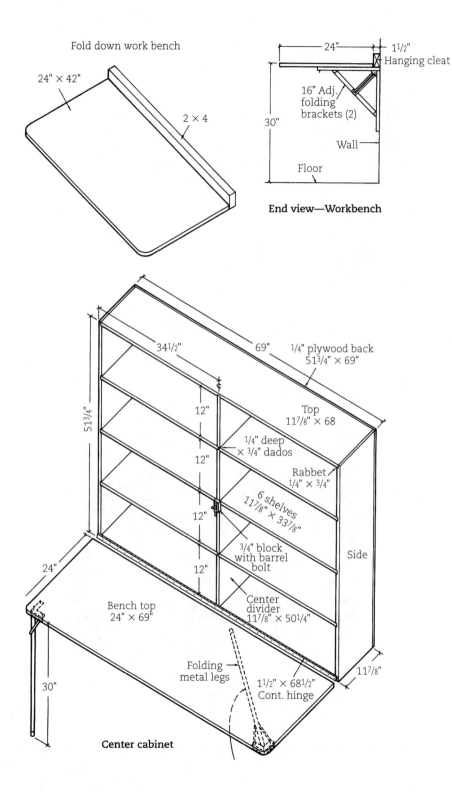

24"

1½"

Hanging cleat

16" Adj. folding brackets (2)

30"

Wall

Floor

**End view—Workbench**

34½"

69"

¼" plywood back
51¾" × 69"

12"

Top
11⅞" × 68

51¾"

¼" deep × ¾" dados

12"

Rabbet
¼" × ¾"

6 shelves
11⅞" × 33⅞"

12"

¾" block with barrel bolt

Side

24"

12"

Bench top
24" × 69"

Center divider
11⅞" × 50¼"

Folding metal legs

30"

1½" × 68½"
Cont. hinge

11⅞"

**Center cabinet**

Fold-out work centers are handy, especially for areas with little maneuvering room, like one-car garages.

Mobile work centers are very versatile. They can be outfitted with an assortment of tools and supplies, and then carted out to work sites. Use one in the garage for auto maintenance, another in the office for files, one in the sewing room for material storage, and so on. Call or write Western Wood Products Association for reasonably priced plans.

Just as the amount of space plays a vital role in accomplishing a task, storing materials safely and conveniently assists goal attainment. Take advantage of the many options available to you, and purchase plans that show how to build durable storage units.

The following set of plans for a Mobile Baking Center can easily be altered to suit a host of other applications.

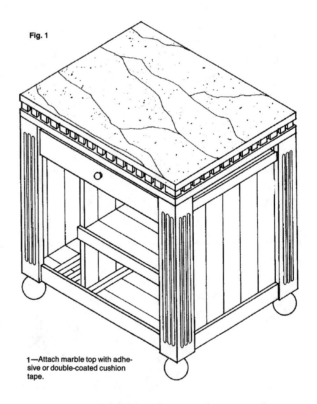

Fig. 1

1—Attach marble top with adhesive or double-coated cushion tape.

**Fig. 2**

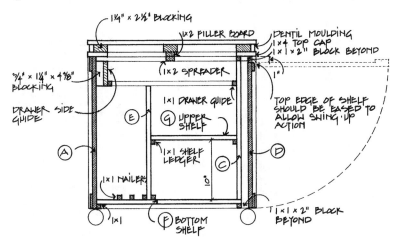

1¼" × 2½" BLOCKING

1×2 FILLER BOARD

DENTIL MOULDING
1×4 TOP CAP
1×1×2" BLOCK BEYOND

¾" × 1¼" × 4⅞" BLOCKING

1×2 SPREADER

1"

DRAWER SIDE GUIDE

1×1 DRAWER GUIDE

Ⓔ

Ⓖ UPPER SHELF

TOP EDGE OF SHELF SHOULD BE EASED TO ALLOW SWING-UP ACTION

Ⓐ

1×1 SHELF LEDGER

Ⓒ

Ⓓ

10"

1×1 NAILERS

Ⓕ BOTTOM SHELF

1×1×2" BLOCK BEYOND

1×1

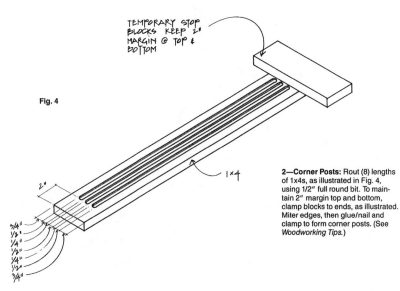

TEMPORARY STOP BLOCKS KEEP 2" MARGIN @ TOP & BOTTOM

**Fig. 4**

1×4

2"

¾"
½"
¼"
½"
¼"
½"
¾"

**2—Corner Posts:** Rout (8) lengths of 1x4s, as illustrated in Fig. 4, using 1/2" full round bit. To maintain 2" margin top and bottom, clamp blocks to ends, as illustrated. Miter edges, then glue/nail and clamp to form corner posts. (See *Woodworking Tips.*)

Work & craft centers    113

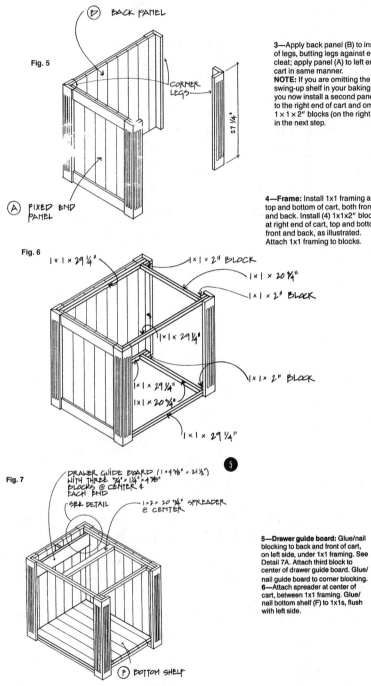

**Fig. 5**

Ⓑ BACK PANEL

CORNER LEGS

27 1/4"

Ⓐ FIXED END PANEL

**3**—Apply back panel (B) to inside of legs, butting legs against end of cleat; apply panel (A) to left end of cart in same manner.
**NOTE:** If you are omitting the swing-up shelf in your baking cart, you now install a second panel (A) to the right end of cart and omit the 1 x 1 x 2″ blocks (on the right end) in the next step.

**4**—**Frame:** Install 1x1 framing at top and bottom of cart, both front and back. Install (4) 1x1x2″ blocks at right end of cart, top and bottom, front and back, as illustrated. Attach 1x1 framing to blocks.

**Fig. 6**

1 x 1 x 29 1/4"

1 x 1 x 2" BLOCK

1 x 1 x 20 3/4"

1 x 1 x 2" BLOCK

1 x 1 x 29 1/4"

1 x 1 x 2" BLOCK

1 x 1 x 29 1/4"

1 x 1 x 20 3/4"

1 x 1 x 29 1/4"

**Fig. 7**

5

DRAWER GUIDE BOARD (1 x 4 3/8" x 21 1/2") WITH THREE 3/4" x 1 1/4" x 4 3/8" BLOCKS @ CENTER & EACH END

SEE DETAIL

1 x 2 x 20 3/4" SPREADER @ CENTER

**5**—**Drawer guide board:** Glue/nail blocking to back and front of cart, on left side, under 1x1 framing. See Detail 7A. Attach third block to center of drawer guide board. Glue/nail guide board to corner blocking.
**6**—Attach spreader at center of cart, between 1x1 framing. Glue/nail bottom shelf (F) to 1x1s, flush with left side.

Ⓕ BOTTOM SHELF

114   Home office, work, and utility spaces

**Fig. 8**

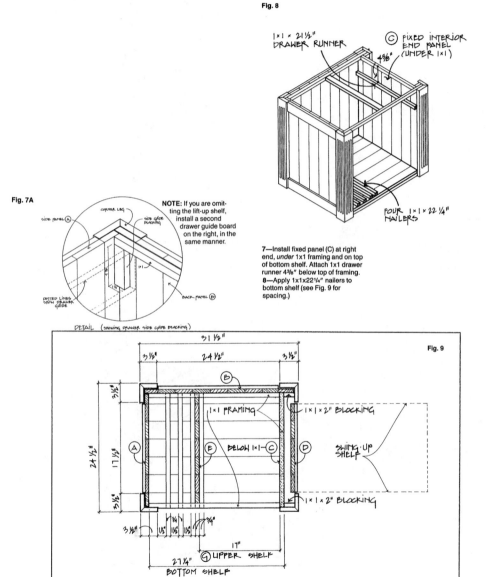

1×1 × 21½"
DRAWER RUNNER

Ⓒ FIXED INTERIOR
END PANEL
(UNDER 1×1)

4⅜"

FOUR 1×1× 22¼"
NAILERS

**Fig. 7A**

SIDE PANEL Ⓐ

CORNER LEG

SIDE GUIDE BLOCKING

1×1

DOTTED LINES SHOW DRAWER GUIDE

BACK PANEL Ⓓ

DETAIL (SHOWING DRAWER SIDE GUIDE BLOCKING)

**NOTE:** If you are omitting the lift-up shelf, install a second drawer guide board on the right, in the same manner.

7—Install fixed panel (C) at right end, *under* 1x1 framing and on top of bottom shelf. Attach 1x1 drawer runner 4⅜" below top of framing.
8—Apply 1x1x22¼" nailers to bottom shelf (see Fig. 9 for spacing.)

**Fig. 9**

31½"

3½"    24½"    3½"

Ⓑ

3½"

1×1 FRAMING

1×1×2" BLOCKING

Ⓐ

24½"    17½"

Ⓔ    BELOW 1×1—Ⓒ    Ⓓ

SWING·UP SHELF

3½"

1×1×2" BLOCKING

3½"    1½"  1½"  1½"    ¾"

17"
Ⓕ UPPER SHELF

27¼"
BOTTOM SHELF

Work & craft centers    115

Fig. 10

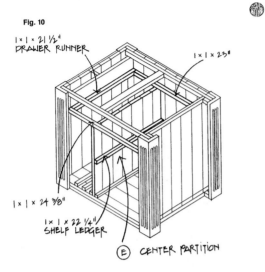

1×1×21½"
DRAWER RUNNER

1×1×23"

1×1×24⅜"

1×1×22¼"
SHELF LEDGER

(E) CENTER PARTITION

**9—**Attach 1x1 drawer runner flush with bottom of drawer guide board (left side). 1x1 is set back 3/4" from front. Apply 1x1 to back panel, in line with drawer runners on either side. Attach front drawer frame to drawer runners on either side.

**10—**Glue/nail 1x1 shelf ledger to center partition (E) and right panel (C) 14" above bottom shelf. Slip partition between nailers; nail to drawer frame at top.

Fig. 12

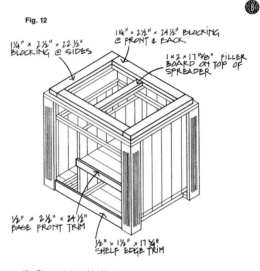

1¼" × 2½" × 22½"
BLOCKING @ SIDES

1¼" × 2½" × 24½" BLOCKING
@ FRONT & BACK

1×2×17⅝" FILLER
BOARD ON TOP OF
SPREADER

½" × 2½" × 24½"
BASE FRONT TRIM

½" × 1½" × 17¾"
SHELF EDGE TRIM

**12—**Glue and clamp blocking to top at front, back and sides. (May be secured with screws.) Inset 1" from edge of top cap. Attach filler board on top of spreader.

Apply bottom trim flush with base of unit; apply shelf trim flush with bottom of shelf. (Note that trim is 1/2" thick.)

Fig. 11

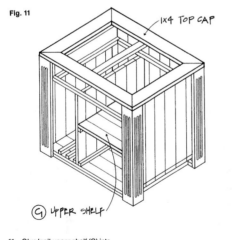

1x4 TOP CAP

(G) UPPER SHELF

**11—**Glue/nail upper shelf (G) into position.

Miter ends of 1x4 top cap and attach to top. Outer edge of top cap is flush with legs.

Fig. 13

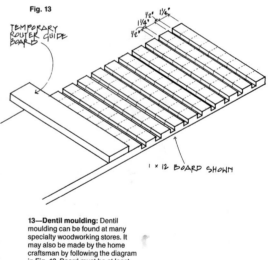

TEMPORARY
ROUTER GUIDE
BOARD

½" 1¼"
¼"
½"

1×12 BOARD SHOWN

**13—Dentil moulding:** Dentil moulding can be found at many specialty woodworking stores. It may also be made by the home craftsman by following the diagram in Fig. 13. Board must be at least 8" wide and 33" long.

Using 1/2" router bit, cut grooves 1¼" apart. (Router guide is clamped in place.) After sanding, rip board into 1¼" wide pieces (see dotted lines).

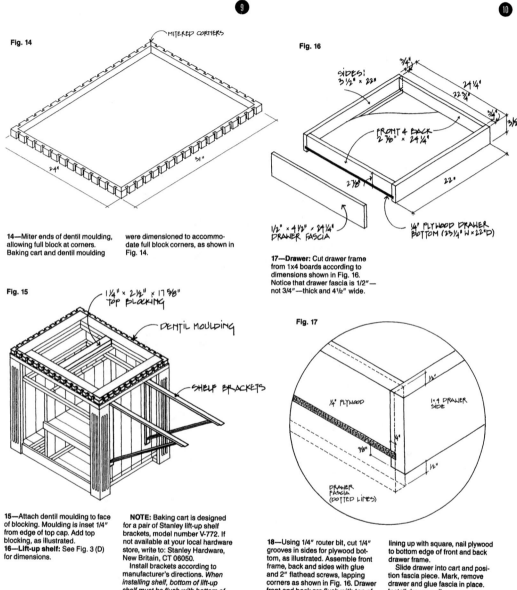

**Fig. 14**

MITERED CORNERS

24"

31"

**Fig. 16**

SIDES!
3½" × 22"

3/4"

24¼"
22¾"

3/4"

FRONT & BACK
2⅞" × 24¼"

3/8"

2⅞"

22"

½" × 4½" × 24¼"
DRAWER FASCIA

¼" PLYWOOD DRAWER
BOTTOM (23¼" W × 22" D)

**Fig. 15**

1¼" × 2½" × 17⅝"
TOP BLOCKING

DENTIL MOULDING

SHELF BRACKETS

**Fig. 17**

¼" PLYWOOD

1×4 DRAWER
SIDE

3/8"

DRAWER
FASCIA
(DOTTED LINES)

½"

½"

**14**—Miter ends of dentil moulding, allowing full block at corners. Baking cart and dentil moulding

were dimensioned to accommodate full block corners, as shown in Fig. 14.

**15**—Attach dentil moulding to face of blocking. Moulding is inset 1/4″ from edge of top cap. Add top blocking, as illustrated.
**16—Lift-up shelf:** See Fig. 3 (D) for dimensions.

**NOTE:** Baking cart is designed for a pair of Stanley lift-up shelf brackets, model number V-772. If not available at your local hardware store, write to: Stanley Hardware, New Britain, CT 06050.

Install brackets according to manufacturer's directions. *When installing shelf, bottom of lift-up shelf must be flush with bottom of baking cart.* (See Fig. 2) This leaves a 1″ space at top to accommodate shelf in raised position. Ease top edge of shelf to allow swing-up action.

**17—Drawer:** Cut drawer frame from 1x4 boards according to dimensions shown in Fig. 16. Notice that drawer fascia is 1/2″—not 3/4″—thick and 4½″ wide.

**18**—Using 1/4″ router bit, cut 1/4″ grooves in sides for plywood bottom, as illustrated. Assemble front frame, back and sides with glue and 2″ flathead screws, lapping corners as shown in Fig. 16. Drawer front and back are flush with top of grooves.

Apply glue to grooves and slide 1/4″ plywood into grooves. After

lining up with square, nail plywood to bottom edge of front and back drawer frame.

Slide drawer into cart and position fascia piece. Mark, remove drawer and glue fascia in place. Install drawer pull.
**19**—Turn cart upside down and install casters.

Work & craft centers   117

**Fig. A**

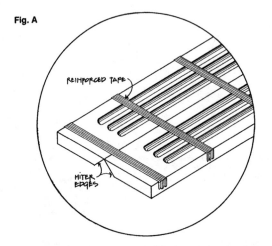

REINFORCED TAPE

MITER EDGES

If you have a problem clamping long miters, such as on the baking cart legs, here's an easy solution:

After cutting miter and gluing edges, apply reinforced tape (packing tape) to outside every 6″ to 8″, as shown. Allow enough extra tape to extend across opening (Fig. B).

Draw mitered edges together and nail from both sides. Draw remaining tape across opening and "clamp" joint until glue dries.

**Fig. B**

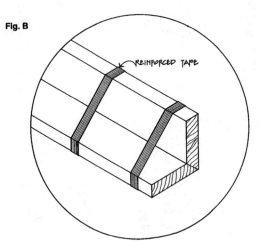

REINFORCED TAPE

118   Home office, work, and utility spaces

# Counters

## CHAPTER 9

MOBILE WORK CENTERS, CARTS, AND STATIONS might be fine for some applications. However, permanent work counters, with storage cabinet spaces below and open worktops above, serve as the center for the majority of endeavors in home tasks or projects.

The term *counters* might initially conjure thoughts of plain-looking work centers appropriate for commercial applications. But once again, you must realize that basic counters are built and assembled in the same way as extravagant ones. Differences in design primarily relate to the materials used in construction, trim and molding options, the incorporation of open areas to accommodate chairs, height, and so on.

Put together a series of base cabinet units made of ¾-inch hardwood plywood, build them to a height of 27 to 29 inches, install a solid-wood top, leave a 24- to 36-inch-wide opening in the middle, seal and stain it to a rich hue, and you will have a beautiful, efficient office/work center. Use particleboard and cover all surface areas with a plastic laminate, and you'll have a versatile sewing or craft center. Build base units taller and install a deeper top, and you'll have a drafting table center with abundant storage beneath that is comfortable to work at while sitting on a stool.

Once you have learned how basic counters are constructed, use your imagination to build units that will satisfy your needs and space options. Be sure to measure all of the tools, materials, and supplies you expect to store in your new work center so that cabinets and drawers will easily accommodate them. At the same time, ensure that the counter height will serve you comfortably while you sit or stand.

What's the difference between a cabinet and a counter? A cabinet is mainly a storage unit secured to a wall that goes from the floor to the ceiling and has no worktop, while a counter is simply a cabinet with a worktop.

## Basic counter/cabinet construction

This sink/counter unit consists of ¾-inch ACX plywood panels, 1-x-2 Douglas fir rails and stiles, ¾-inch birch plywood doors and drawer fronts, and a prefabricated particleboard/laminate top. At 24 inches deep and 60 inches long, it was built to fit in a corner of a utility bathroom/darkroom. At 36 inches in height, the unit comfortably accommodates users while they stand during film processing. The prefabricated top cost just over $20 at a home improvement center—about a third of what it would have cost to purchase a 4-x-8 sheet of ¾-inch particleboard and a 4-x-8 sheet of laminate for a homemade top.

These counters will be connected with small screws through one stile and into the other in a corner of a home utility center. The upper framework is made with a 2-x-2 top front rail and 2-x-4 horizontal blocks between the front rail and rear cleat. They will serve as a sturdy network of braces for the sometimes heavy repair tasks that will grace the countertops. A #8 3-inch screw is being driven through the top front frame rail. The rail will be covered in front with an attractive piece of Douglas fir as part of the unit's front rail and stile finish.

Base counter units are constructed like cupboards; plywood end panels support a floor and inner shelves. Framing on the top holds units together and serves as supports for countertops. Base cabinets can be made in separate units up to 4 feet wide, and then connected together to form long counters. Or, build them up to 8 feet long (the full length of plywood sheets) to fit along wide walls.

If you don't have a panel saw, cut plywood with a circular saw and guide as it rests securely on top of four 2 × 4s. Place two 2 × 4s on each side of cuts so that both plywood halves remain evenly supported during and after cutting operations.

Lower front counter sections must be provided with a toe kick, an open area at floor level that allows feet to fit slightly under counter fronts to make standing at them more comfortable. Without toe kicks, people would have to stoop while working at counters. This is an uncomfortable and awkward position. Toe kicks generally measure about 4 inches deep and 3½ inches high. A 3½-inch height allows for 2-x-4 runners to be installed at the bottom rear and just behind toe kicks to serve as sturdy base supports.

These are two end panels that will be used for a small sink/counter in a laundry room. Both have been sandwiched together and are secured with clamps while a 4-x-3½-inch toe kick section is cut out. Because outer panels will not be visible, ¾-inch ACX plywood is used with the A-sides facing in. The unit will be located in a corner to hide one side. A washing machine will be placed on the other side.

A ¾-inch straight router bit was used to make a dado groove at the bottom of this end panel. Notice that the unit's floor will rest at the top of the toe kick space. Take your time when adjusting routers; make test cuts on a piece of scrap wood to

verify that the cuts are made only as deep as you want. In this case, depth of cut is ⅜ inch, half the thickness of the ¾-inch plywood material. Clamp a straight piece of wood on panels to serve as a router guide. Position the wood guide to account for the distance between the edge of the router bit and edge of the router's base plate.

With an end panel resting on its back, the floor groove was coated with wood glue (on previous page) before the end of the floor was inserted into it. A square was used as a guide to make a pencil line on the outside of the panel, in line with the center of the floor groove on the inside. This line designates the center of the groove to accurately show where nails should be driven. The same process was conducted on the other end panel. Thus, the floor was permanently attached to both panels.

The counter unit rests on its back as a 2-x-4 runner is glued and fastened with #8 2-inch screws to the lower rear corner. Another 2 × 4 will be glued and screwed to the front lower edge. These 2 × 4s serve as sturdy supports for the entire unit. Notice the toe kick cut out at the top of the photo.

The counter's floor and 2-x-4 runners have been glued and screwed in place. Here, a piece of 1-x-4 fir is glued and screwed in place with #8 2-inch screws. This 1-x-4 cleat helps to hold the unit together, and will serve as a support for the top. It will also be the part of the counter's frame that is screwed to the wall to keep the unit firmly anchored in position.

A similar 1-x-2 or 2-x-2 brace could be added to the top front edge for added support. However, since this counter is small, measuring only 30 inches wide and 24 inches deep, an oak 1-x-2 top front rail will suffice. Had the unit been any bigger, or if it was expected to support more weight, a top front frame support would certainly have been installed.

This small counter/sink unit is now starting to take shape. Oak rails and stiles are now ready for installation. Glue will be spread on the plywood panel edges, and the 1-x-2 boards secured to them with 2½-inch finishing nails.

As mentioned earlier, rails and stiles are attached to each other in different fashions. Lap joints, tenon and mortises, biscuits, and other methods are commonly employed by craftsmen of fine furniture. One of the more common and easier to accomplish methods entails the use of a metal block that is outfitted with pre-drilled holes made at a specific angle. That block is clamped in place to serve as a guide to drill wide holes in work pieces. The block is then removed, and a smaller drill bit used to make pilot holes. Afterward, screws are driven through one work piece and into the other for a solid connection.

Rails and stiles are secured to counter units just as they are for bookcases, cupboards and other pieces. Be sure to spread plenty of glue on panel edges before nailing rails and stiles in place. Wipe away excess glue that seeps out from under boards with a clean damp rag. Set nails, place a drop of glue in nail

holes, wipe away excess glue, and then sand the areas as an easy method for filling nail holes and hiding nails.

Pieces of hardwood cut at a 45-degree angle are glued and screwed into the top corners of counter units. These braces help units remain square and sturdy. Screws are inserted from the outside on panel and framework pieces that will not be visible. For front rails, insert screws from the inside. Drill a hole through the tops of angle braces wide enough for a short screw to fit through. Screws will be driven through these holes and into the countertops to hold them in place.

This unit is now ready for a top, drawer front, and doors. Since a sink will be installed in this unit, a drawer will not be made for it. Instead, a drawer front will be secured over the hole to make the unit look complete. Notice that plywood A-sides all face inside, with C-sides facing out.

Had this unit been designed to stand alone in an office as a small work counter, ¾-inch AB grade hardwood plywood would have been used with the A-sides facing out on end panels, and facing in for the floor.

The only difference between this small base cabinet/counter unit and larger ones is the absence of a top front frame member and a network of cross braces going from front to back along the top. For larger units, and those scheduled for a series of drawers, rails and stiles would have to be cut and positioned according to the drawer and cabinet openings designed. Rail and stile positions will determine width and length dimensions for drawers and door openings.

## Cabinet doors & drawer fronts

Making cabinet doors and drawer fronts out of hardwood plywood is relatively easy. However, building beautiful raised-panel doors requires time, experience, and attention to detail. If you have little experience in fine cabinetmaking, you might be best off and most satisfied by purchasing solid-wood doors and drawer fronts. This 6-foot-long counter unit was made with plywood and faced with solid oak rails and stiles. Here, doors and drawer fronts are being installed.

Because plywood edges might not always be perfect, even with hardwood materials, it is usually best if only a portion of these edges remain visible while doors and drawers are closed. For that reason, plan to rabbet plywood door and drawer front edges ⅜ inch wide and ⅜ inch deep so that their edges fit partially into openings.

This style of door edge also helps to keep dust and dirt out of cabinet and drawer areas. Doors and drawer fronts are initially cut ¾ inch wider and longer than their openings to accommodate for rabbeted edges. Always test router adjustments on a piece of scrap wood before using the router on finish materials.

Shapers are heavy-duty machines that function just like routers mounted upside down. A number of shaper cutter heads are available; some will cut a rabbet on one side of plywood door edges and round off the other side in one pass. Here, a round cutter head is employed to effect a round edge on a plywood drawer front.

Doors are easiest to install while base units rest on their back sides. This little counter is starting to look pretty good.

A very wide assortment of cabinet door hinges are available through home improvement centers. There are certain advantages to each style. You must decide which will work and look the best for your application needs. Rabbeted doors require special hinges. One side is shaped at angles to fit around rabbets. For this unit, ⅜-inch rabbet hinges are employed since the door rabbets are ⅜ inch deep and wide.

Hinges are generally placed from 2 inches to 4 inches down from door tops and up from door bottoms; it depends on the size of the door. Place hinges closer to door tops and bottoms for short doors and 4 inches from edges on long doors. Place hinges on doors first by using a screw set to make a pilot hole in one screw opening. Insert a screw and just barely drive it down. Adjust the hinge as necessary to ensure that it sits correctly, and then insert the second and third screws.

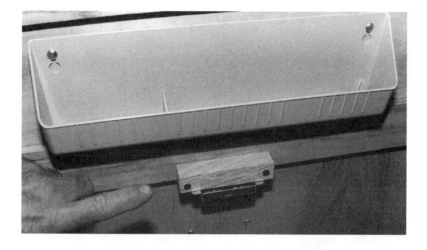

Magnetic door catches do a great job of keeping doors in place while they are closed. Since these rabbeted doors covered a good portion of the bottom of the top rail, a block of wood was installed on the inside of the top rail to serve as a base for this double door magnetic catch. The catch was mounted to the bottom of the block, and small metal plates were screwed to each door. When the doors close, magnets pull on the plates to keep the doors shut.

This base cabinet/counter unit has now been finished, with a piece of oak glued and nailed across the front of the toe kick space. This board covers the plywood end panel edges and the 2-x-4 front runner.

## Countertops

Finished countertops can extend past base cabinet fronts by as little as the width of trim attached to the top's edge to as much as you want; it all depends on how countertops will be used. If they stick out too far, you will not be able to easily retrieve things out of top drawers. However, if you desire a countertop similar to those on drafting tables, one that provides both abundant storage underneath and accommodations for users to work at the counter while sitting on stools, allow the countertop to stick out 6 to 12 inches and do not install top drawers. Build taller cabinet doors, instead.

A small section of ¾-inch particleboard will be cut from this full sheet and used as a top for the small counter/sink unit. The metal cutting guide will be clamped in place to keep a circular saw on course. Countertops are most often fabricated from ¾-inch particleboard and then covered with a laminate material.

Laminates are available in all sorts of colors and designs. For a rich-looking office, you might opt for ¾ inch or thicker hardwood plywood in lieu of particleboard and laminate.

A 2-inch-wide strip has been glued and nailed on the front edge of this top. Be sure cuts are made square and that strips like this rest flush with countertop surfaces. Use a sander as necessary to ensure a flush joint.

A 4-x-8 sheet of almond-colored laminate rested on its finished side while a small section was cut from it. Laminate was cut face down because the little Makita Trim Saw used for this task cuts from the bottom up. Saw blade teeth should enter workpieces on their best side and exit through the other. Always cut laminate about 1 inch wider and longer than required. Never cut it to fit, because saw blades will leave behind jagged, chipped edges. Finish trimming with a laminate-cutting router or trimmer bit, and you'll have perfect edges.

Laminate is secured to particleboard or very smooth AC plywood surfaces with contact cement. After test fitting laminate to ensure it is wider and longer than needed, apply contact cement to both the wood countertop and back side of the laminate according to label instructions. Allow laminate to cure for about 15 minutes.

**Caution:** Contact cement is very flammable! Before using this compound, be certain your work area is free from all ignition sources, like pilot lights for hot water heaters, clothes dryers, stoves, and heaters. Absolutely prohibit all smoking in the area.

Contact cement is designed to adhere to itself. In other words, applying a coat to just one surface and not the other won't work. Therefore, installers place thin strips of wood on

countertops. Then the laminate is placed on top, adjusted, and accurately positioned. Once laminate has been appropriately located, strips are pulled out one at a time and the laminate makes contact with the wood top.

Take pains to ensure wood strips are sliver-free. Small chunks of wood that fall off while strips are pulled away will cause lumps in laminate surfaces. If you don't have softwood strips, use hardwood or slats from old window blinds.

Once contact cement on laminate makes contact with the coated countertop, a permanent bond is made. You will not be able to move laminate in any direction. So if you goofed in its positioning, too bad. That is why you must cut laminate wider and longer than needed and utilize thin wood strips for initial placement.

After laminate has been placed on a countertop and all wood strips are removed, use a 3-inch-wide rubber laminate roller to press laminate down on the wood surface and remove any trapped air bubbles. Work from the center outward. Notice that

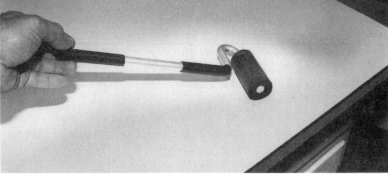

138   Home office, work, and utility spaces

this piece of laminate extends almost an inch past the front edge of the countertop.

A straight carbide-tipped laminate bit has been secured in this Makita Trimmer. Notice that the bit is equipped with a roller at its tip. The tool and bit were used to trim the laminate flush with the edge of the countertop. Operate bits in a direction that allows bit teeth to cut into the work from the countertop toward the outside—not from the outside inward. This ensures that bits cut smoothly and leave behind no jagged edges.

On the previous page, a small piece of laminate was cut for the front trim piece. As with the main countertop, it was cut bigger and wider than necessary. Contact cement was placed on both the trim piece and laminate; it rested for 15 minutes, plenty of time for the cement to cure and lose its initial glossy sheen.

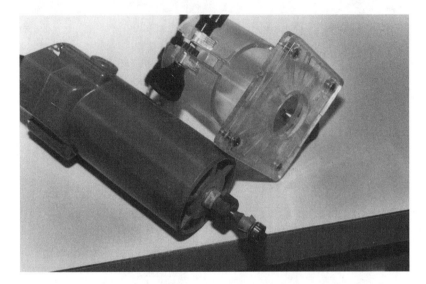

A straight laminate bit was used to trim the bottom and sides of this front trim piece. On the top edge, a 15-degree carbide-tipped laminate bit was employed. The clear trimmer base was removed only for this photo so that the 15-degree laminate bit could be easily recognized. Take time in adjusting the depth of cut for this bit to ensure an attractive and professional-looking finished trimming job.

Trim could have continued around the top of this unit if it were to be used in an open area with sides completely visible. As it is, the right side of this unit will rest against a wall and the left side will be hidden by a washing machine.

Longer counter base units are installed and secured in place first. Afterward, tops are attached and then covered with laminate.

With the top removed, this unit is installed in a corner of the new laundry/sewing room. A level is used to help determine

correct positioning. Thin shims might be necessary along 2-x-4 floor runners to adjust units and make them level. Check to be sure units are level in all directions.

Since few walls are ever perfectly flat, you might need to place wood shims between them and the back sides of top rear cleats. With this unit level, shims were positioned in place and pilot holes drilled for #8 2½-inch screws that were then driven through the cleat and into wall studs. With that job done, the top was put on and then secured with screws driven from the bottom through the 45-degree corner braces.

## Drawers

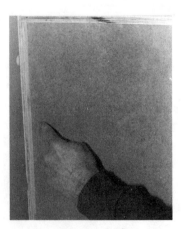

Drawers are simply small boxes made from ½-inch ACX plywood, hardwood plywood, or other ½- or ¾-inch-thick solid wood. Drawer bottoms might consist of hardboard, ¼- or ³⁄₁₆-inch plywood, or other comparable material.

Dado grooves ¼ inch deep were cut along the bottoms of these drawer sides. A piece of ¼-inch hardboard has been slipped into the grooves. Drawer bottoms are not generally secured in place with glue or nails; they are left to float freely. Dado grooves are made about ½ inch up from the bottom edge of drawer sides.

All four drawer sides are dadoed for the drawer bottoms and the ends of the side pieces rabbeted to make solid joints. Three sides are glued and nailed together. Then the bottom is slipped

into place before the fourth side is attached. Once the basic unit has been completed, an attractive drawer front is secured to the working front with short screws driven from inside.

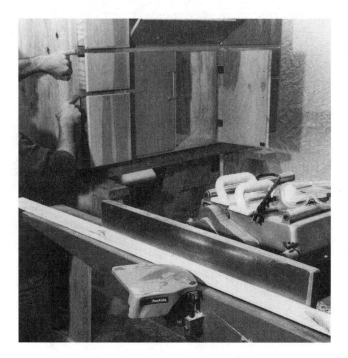

Drawer ends are cut at least ½ inch shorter than cabinet openings provided by rails and stiles, which allows room for them to be maneuvered into place on drawer guides. Drawer dimensions are critical with regard to certain types of drawer guides. Made too wide, too narrow, or too tall, drawers might not fit into spaces at all, could wobble when operated, or be too tight-fitting to slide back and forth easily. Therefore, carefully read and follow drawer guide installation instructions before building drawers.

## Summary

Counters make excellent home work centers. To incorporate desks between base cabinets, simply allow sections of countertops to span open areas between base units. Attach drawer guides to base units on both sides of the opening to support drawers, or install computer keyboard trays in that space. Mount them to countertop bottom sides.

With regard to countertop height, be certain base cabinet heights take into account the thickness of countertop material so that the finished unit will rest at the overall height you originally desired. For a lowered typewriter work top, just install cleats to the sides of base cabinets and secure a finished work top on them. Desk areas like these are commonly built into many kitchen/family room counters.

# Laundry & sewing room conveniences

## CHAPTER 10

MANY HOMEOWNERS SUCCESSFULLY wash and dry clothes in garages. Those with interests in sewing have made beautiful outfits at kitchen tables. However, they would probably admit that having a utility room or actual laundry/sewing space would be wonderful.

Outfitted with cupboards and counters, laundry and sewing rooms are sufficient. Adding some conveniences, though, would make them even better. Seriously consider the regular activities that will take place in laundry and sewing rooms, and strive to outfit them with hooks, bulletin boards, pegboard areas, and other devices that will assist you in making those spaces as efficient and practical as possible.

Laundry and sewing areas are frequently combined in a home. After all, activities in each place are related to the same thing—clothing. Although a small, private sewing area in an attic space or other room in a house might be preferred by some, it might be most convenient to combine laundry and sewing functions in one room. Try to keep both service areas somewhat separated, though, so that clothes folding (for example) does not interfere with sewing projects underway.

A clothes washer and dryer on one side of the room, with a folding table next to the dryer, help to keep clothes away from the active sewing center across the room. Dirty clothes hampers could be stored under the folding table.

Combination laundry/sewing room floor plans will be dictated to some degree by the locations of doors and plumbing utilities. Washers must be stationed on a wall that can be practically served with a drain pipe; fresh water can be routed in most any direction. On the same token, clothes dryers must exhaust to

## Floor plan ideas

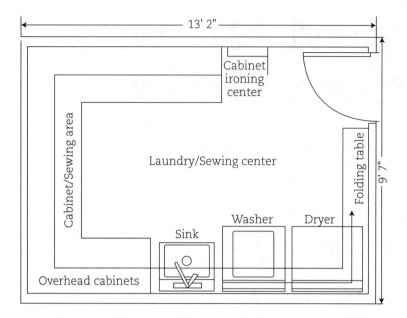

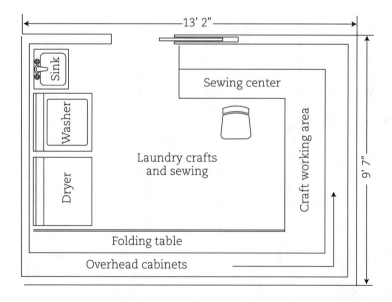

the outdoors, and exhaust tubing cannot extend more than 25 feet in a straight line. Drain pipes and dryer exhausts, therefore, are primary laundry room concerns.

Utility sinks are one of the most convenient laundry room accessories. Filthy clothes are rinsed in them before being put into washing machines. Stained garments could soak in these sinks; once you have one, you'll wonder how you ever got along without it.

## Laundry room sink installation

Utility sink drains are connected to ABS plastic drain pipe with ABS glue. In most cases, sink drain piping is 1½ inches in diameter and drain pipes in walls are 2 inches in diameter. Therefore, a 2- to 1½-inch reducer fitting will have to be connected to the drain stub that exits the wall. Connectors like this one feature a 2-inch female opening that is glued to 2-inch wall drain pipe stubs. On the other end, these fittings feature a threaded male 1½-inch-diameter pipe extension.

The Vanity Installation Kit from PlumbShop on the following page includes all of the fittings needed to make a complete sink hookup, including the P-trap and other drain fittings and pipe

except the 2- to 1½-inch threaded reducer. Fresh hot and cold water pipe nipples are outfitted with valves so that water can be turned off if faucets leak and need repair. All fresh water threaded pipe connections must be sealed with wraps of Teflon pipe tape over male threads.

Make initial drain and fresh water pipe connections at the wall first, before securing a new sink or sink top in place over the counter. You'll enjoy working without a sink in the way.

The installation instructions for this stainless steel utility sink are very clear and concise. This sink has been placed upside down on the countertop and positioned squarely with regard to all four countertop sides. A pencil line was then drawn around the entire sink circumference to serve as a preliminary reference for cutting out a section of the countertop to make way for the sink.

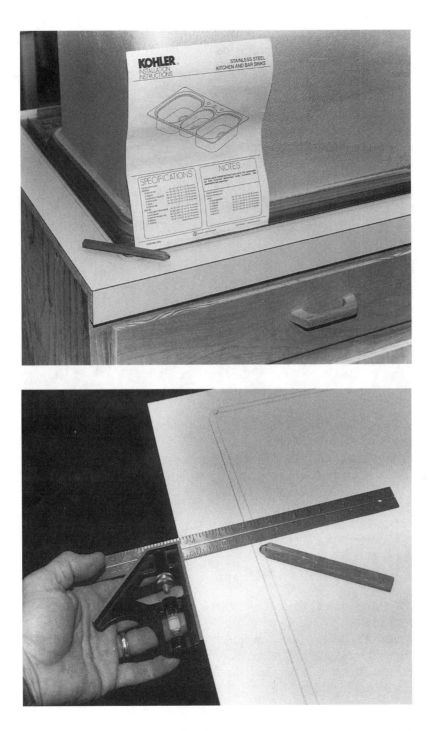

Next, a combination square was set up to assist in drawing another pencil line ¼ inch inside the first. Actual cutting will take place on the inside line; if it was done on the outside line, the sink would just fall through the opening.

A ½-inch hole was drilled just to the inside of the inner pencil line. It makes room for the insertion of a jig saw blade. A jig saw is used to cut out this section of countertop. Making cuts around tight corners might require a few separate passes.

Remember that extra cutting to help jig saws maneuver around corners must be done toward the middle of the countertop. The section being cut out is waste material; the areas closer toward the outer pencil line will be the parts that actually support the sink.

After a section of the countertop has been cut out to make room for the sink, set the sink on a table or bench and assemble its faucet. Follow instructions closely and be sure to wrap all male threads with Teflon pipe tape before connecting them to their mates. This faucet system includes a handy spray nozzle; its hose is coiled up tight to facilitate the sink installation.

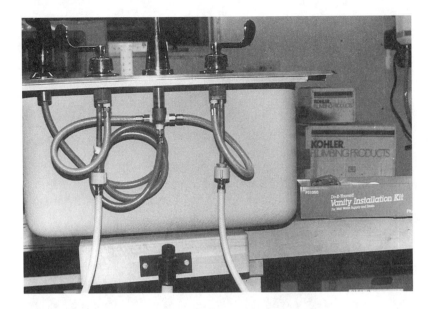

Laundry & sewing room conveniences     151

According to instructions, install J-hooks around the sink lip inside a channel designed for them. After installation, turn them to the side so they will fit through the sink opening in the counter. Once you are ready to actually put the sink in place, put down a bead of caulk around the sink edge as on previous page. This bead will make a seal between the sink lip and countertop, making it watertight. Note: Almond-colored caulking was used in this application because the countertop is almond.

Place the sink in position on the countertop, adjust as necessary, and wipe away excess caulking with a clean damp cloth. Then twist J-hook lips over the bottom of the countertop opening and secure them in place by tightening the nuts located on threaded hook shafts.

After the sink has been secured to the countertop, you will be ready to make up the drain connection. Place a bead of plumber's putty around the drain flange so it will maintain a watertight seal between the drain and sink bottom. From below, slip on the rubber and plastic washers and then secure the unit in place with its large drain nut.

A tail piece is connected to the drain with its own large nut. Drain pipe from the Vanity Installation Kit is secured with a washer and plastic nut to the bottom end of the tail piece. The

P-trap connects to it, and more pipe is run to the wall drain and connected to the threaded wall drain pipe with another plastic nut. Depending upon the installation, tail pieces and/or horizontal running pipe may have to be cut to fit. For other projects, you might need a longer tail piece. They are available at home improvement centers and plumbing shops.

On the fresh water side, wrap Teflon tape around the male threads on valves and connect the faucet supply hoses. Be sure that the hot and cold water hoses are correctly connected to the appropriate hot and cold water valves. Convinced that your job is complete, turn on the water and check for leaks.

Although the following convenience items are featured in a laundry room setting, you should understand that any of them could be used throughout a home as needed.

## Other conveniences

Häfele America Company offers a wide range of different trays, baskets, and containers designed to fit inside counters and cabinets. They can be used for almost any storage need. Here, a set of two plastic pails are supported by a frame that is screwed to counter floors. Pails slide out on guides. As they do, the top lifts up. Pails simply lift out of the frame for emptying.

This unit is supported by two sliders that are mounted to the side of a counter or cabinet. Since the stile on this counter extends into the opening by ¾ inch, two ¾-inch-thick boards will be secured to the counter with #6 1¼-inch screws. The tray will be secured to them.

The sliding storage tray on the left will hold cleansers, liquid soap, sponges, and so on, under a utility sink.

The sliding storage tray on the next page is large. Its frame mounts to a counter or cabinet floor with screws. One basket is removable, making it handy for carrying cleaning or other supplies to different locations. This tray could also be useful in craft or sewing areas when positioned in a cabinet space located next to a desk or work area.

Corner cabinets in almost any room are notorious for wasted space. A logical solution to that waste is a "lazy susan": a large unit that features two big shelves and a quarter cut at the front. The assembly would sit behind two separate 1-foot-wide doors. A template is included to assist installers in locating the correct position for the unit's base plate.

Brooms, mops, and other odd-shaped household items are easy to store securely and out of the way with this unit. Two hooks wedge themselves against handles as the weight of objects puts stress on them. When the unit is mounted on pegboard, other items can also be stored nearby.

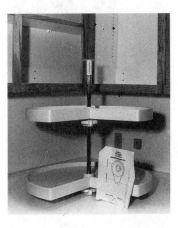

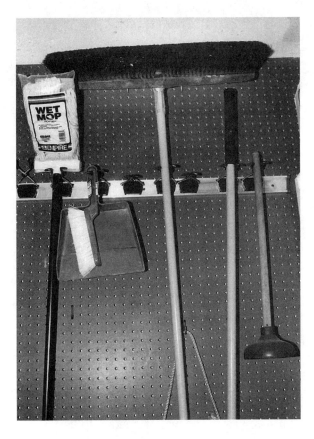

One of the more frustrating storage problems frequently found in laundry rooms involves idle clothes hangers. One simple solution employs the use of a closet rod suspended from the bottom of an upper cupboard. Here, a Makita Self-Feed drill bit is used on a drill press to bore a 1¼-inch hole partially into a block of oak. Another hole will be drilled into a second oak block. This size hole was made to accommodate a 1¼-inch-diameter closet rod (large wood dowel).

Next, the oak blocks were secured to a workbench. A round bit was used on a router to round off all edges. This was done for appearance only. Notice that the far end of the blocks are not routed. They will remain square in order to fit tight against the bottom of a cupboard.

Oak blocks were secured to the bottom of this cupboard with #8 2½-inch screws. Pilot and countersink holes were drilled first to prevent oak from cracking and to allow screw heads to rest flush against the surface of the shelf.

Before this clothes hanger rod was made or installed, measurements were taken on the washer and dryer that will occupy this space. That was done to ensure that the clothes hangers would not interfere with opening or closing the washing machine lid. A clothes hanger was used to determine how far down from the cupboard the closet rod should hang, and how far away from the wall it needed to be.

NuTone's built-in ironing center can be installed in walls between studs or surface mounted on wall faces. This oak frame is used for surface-mount applications. All of the parts and screws are contained in the package to make a surface-mount installation very simple. Optional doors are available for this unit in solid wood and mirror models.

## Built-in ironing center

During the vacated bedroom/new laundry room remodeling process, a section of wall was framed to accommodate the NuTone ironing center. As you can see here, a solid section of

drywall was installed on the upper wall and then a section cut out to open up the ironing center space. The same was done for the lower drywall section.

This opening was built to the dimensions specified in the installation instructions for the ironing center. The 12/2 with ground wires above have not been connected to a power source yet; they have just been routed and secured in position. One wire will supply power to the ironing center by way of a 20-amp circuit. The other wire runs to an outlet nearby. Both will be connected to the ironing center wiring with wire nuts inside the electrical connection box on the ironing center.

The ironing center fits into its space like a glove. An angle drill was used to drill pilot holes into the studs through holes provided on the ironing center frame. Large Phillips-head screws secure the unit in place.

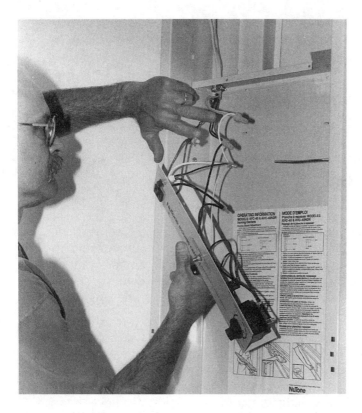

A panel was removed from the top left corner of the unit for electrical wire access. The control box was dislodged by loosening two screws. White wires were connected together with wire nuts. The black wires were connected to black, and ground to ground. This control box includes a 50-watt light fixture, an electrical outlet for the iron, and two safety devices. One is a timer that automaticlaly switches an iron off after a preset time limit, and the other is a power cut-off button which is activated each time the ironing board is locked in its storage position.

Once your laundry and sewing room has been outfitted with cupboards and shelves, cabinets and counters, and all of the other neat storage things you have dreamed about, fill it with quality sewing tools. Make all of your sewing projects flow flawlessly with a pfaff sewing machine and serger.

Because many family members dump loads of dirty clothes in laundry rooms or otherwise leave those areas in disarray, consider having a family meeting to discuss how you could outfit your new laundry/sewing center in a way that would simplify keeping it organized and tidy. You never know, someone might come up with an ingenious idea that could make everyone's eyes sparkle. Once that plan is accomplished, the whole family might want to take over all of the laundry chores! Now, wouldn't that be something?

## Final summary

I hope that the information, photos, and illustrations in this book help you to design and outfit the home office, work, and utility spaces you have always dreamed about. Remember to measure twice and cut once, test router cuts on scrap wood first, and wear safety goggles while striking objects or using any power tools. May your remodeling efforts flow smoothly, result in perfection, and award you with loads of satisfaction.

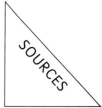

THE COMPANIES AND ORGANIZATIONS listed on this and the following pages have provided information and assistance for this book. My personal experience using tools and pieces of equipment, and installing materials and products from these sources has been outstanding. I highly recommend you contact these companies for catalogs and additional information.

Alta Industries
P.O. Box 2764
Santa Rosa, CA 95405
(707) 544-5009
*tool belts and pouches*

American Plywood Assoc.
P.O. Box 11700
Tacoma, WA 98411
(206) 565-6600
*information and building plans for plywood*

American Tool Co., Inc.
P.O. Box 337
De Witt, NE 68341
(402) 683-2315
*Vise-Grip, Quick-Grip, Prosnip, CHESCO, and more tools*

Autodesk Retail Products
11911 N. Creek Parkway S.
Bothell, WA 98011
(800) 228-3601
*plans-making computer software*

Behr Process Corporation
3400 W. Segerstrom Ave.
Santa Ana, CA 92704
(800) 854-0133
*paint, stain, varnish, sealers, and more*

Campbell Hausfeld
100 Production Dr.
Harrison, OH 45030
(513) 367-4811
*air compressors, pneumatic tools, pressure washers, and more*

Cedar Shake and Shingle Bureau
515 116th Ave. NE, Ste. 275
Bellevue, WA 98004-5294
(206) 453-1323
*information regarding cedar shakes and shingles*

DAP, Inc.
P.O. Box 277
Dayton, OH 45401
(800) 568-4554
*sealants, caulking, adhesives, and more*

Dritz Corp.
P.O. Box 5028
Spartanburg, SC 29304
(803) 576-5050
*sewing devices, tools, and accessories*

Eagle Windows and Doors
375 E. Ninth St.
Dubuque, IA 52004
(319) 556-2270
*high-quality wood windows and doors*

The Eastwood Co.
580 Lancaster Ave., Box 3014
Malvern, PA 19355-0714
(800) 345-1178
*automotive and metalworking
tools and supplies*

Empire Brushes, Inc.
U.S. 13 North
P.O. Box 1606
Greenville, NC 27835-1606
*brushes, brooms, and accessories*

Freud
P.O. Box 7187
High Point, NC 27264
(800) 472-7307
*biscuit cutters and other tools*

General Cable Co. (Romex ®)
4 Tesseneer Dr.
Highland Heights, KY 41076
(606) 572-8000
*electrical wire*

Hafele America Co.
3901 Cheyenne Dr.
P.O. Box 4000
Archdale, NC 27263
(910) 889-2322
*cabinet and furniture hardware of
all types*

Halo Lighting (Cooper
Lighting)
400 Busse Rd.
Elk Grove Village, IL 60007
(708) 956-8400
*recessed ceiling lights*

Harbor Freight Tools (Central
Purchasing, Inc.)
3491 Mission Oaks Blvd.
Camarillo, CA 95008
(800) 423-2567
*home improvement tools,
supplies, and more*

Keller Industries, Inc.
1800 State Rd. Nine
Miami, FL 33162
(800) 222-2600
*ladders, attic stairways, and
accessories*

Kohler Co.
444 Highland Dr.
Kohler, WI 53044
(414) 457-4441
*bathroom fixtures and accessories*

Leslie-Locke, Inc.
4501 Circle 75 Pkwy.
Ste. F-6300
Atlanta, GA 30339
*roof windows, skylights, heat
ducting, and more*

Leviton Manufacturing Co.,
Inc.
59-25 Little Neck Pkwy.
Little Neck, NY 11362-2591
(718) 229-4040
*electrical switches, receptacles,
and more*

Makita USA, Inc.
14930 Northam St.
La Mirada, CA 90638-5753
(714) 522-8088
*power and cordless tools and
equipment*

McGuire-Nicholas Co., Inc.
2331 Tubeway Ave.
City of Commerce, CA 90040
(213) 722-6961
*tool belts, pouches, knee pads, back braces, and more*

NuTone
Madison and Red Bank Rds.
Cincinnati, OH 45227-1599
(800) 543-8687
*built-in convenience products*

Owens-Corning Fiberglas
Insulation
Fiberglas Tower
Toledo, OH 43659
(800) 342-3745
*pink insulation for ceilings, floors, and walls*

PanelLift Telpro, Inc.
Rt. 1, Box 138
Grand Forks, ND 58201
(800) 441-0551
*drywall lift equipment*

PFAFF American Sales Corp.
610 Winters Ave.
P.O. Box 566
Paramus, NJ 07653-0566
(800) 526-0273
*high-quality sewing machines and sergers*

Plano Molding Co.
431 East South St.
Plano, IL 60545-1601
(800) 874-6905
*plastic tool boxes, storage units, shelves, and more*

PlumbShop
(a division of Brass Craft)
39600 Orchard Hill Place
Novi, MI 48376
(810) 305-6000
*plumbing supplies*

Power Products Co. (SIMKAR)
Cayuga and Ramona Sts.
Philadelphia, PA 19120
(800) 346-7833
*fluorescent lighting*

Power Tool Institute, Inc.
1300 Sumner Ave.
Cleveland, OH 44115-2851
(216) 241-7333
*information on safe power tool operations*

Quality Doors
603 Big Stone Gap Rd.
Duncanville, TX 75137
(800) 950-3667
*cabinet doors and refacing materials*

Simpson Strong-Tie Connector
Co., Inc.
1450 Doolittle Dr.
San Leandro, CA 94577
(800) 999-5099
*metal connectors*

The Stanley Works
1000 Stanley Dr.
New Britain, CT 06053
(800) 551-5936
*hand tools, hardware, closet organizers, and more*

Sta-Put Color Pegs
23504 29th Ave. W.
Lynnwood, WA 98036-8318
*plastic pegboard hooks*

Structron Corp.
1980 Diamond St.
San Marcos, CA 92069
(619) 744-6371
*garden and construction tools*

Tyvek (DuPont)
Chestnut Run WR-2058
Wilmington, DE 19880-0722
(800) 448-9835
*Housewrap*

U.S. Ceramic Tile Co.
P.O. Box 338
East Sparta, OH 44626
(216) 866-5531
*ceramic tile*

Weiser Lock
6660 South Broadmoor Rd.
Tucson, AZ 85746
(602) 741-6200
*door locks, handles, and knobs*

Western Wood Products Assoc.
522 SW Fifth Ave.
Portland, OR 97204-2122
*information and building plans*

Zircon Corp.
1580 Dell Avenue
Campbell, CA 95008
(408) 866-8600
*water levels and other devices*